**DATE DUE**

| | | | |
|---|---|---|---|
| | | | |
| | | | |
| | | | |
| | | | |
| | | | |
| | | | |
| | | | |
| | | | |
| | | | |
| | | | |
| | | | |
| | | | |

# THE HOUSE OF WINGS
Betsy Byars

"Liar," Sammy screamed. "Dirty, stinking liar!"

His grandfather took a step and looked down at his feet. "This morning," he said, "your mom and dad was talking about all the trouble they was going to have getting settled in Detroit....Well... it just came about naturally that you would be better off staying with me."

Furious, Sammy ran. Followed doggedly by the old man, who, in the midst of the chase, found a wounded crane. The old man called softly for the boy to come back, and somehow Sammy knew his grandfather was not calling him in order to capture him, but was calling him for something more important than their feud.

Sammy was almost at his grandfather's side before he saw the crane. The old man was standing perfectly still. How Sammy hated him! His life had been changed, and it would never be the same again, and somehow his grandfather was to blame. But there was something about the old man, speaking softly now so that the crane wouldn't run, something about the wounded bird and the stillness all around them. Sammy stayed as if he were rooted to the ground, then moved to help his grandfather catch the crane.

# The House of Wings

BETSY BYARS

Illustrated by
Daniel Schwartz

PUFFIN BOOKS

# For Charlie and Michael

PUFFIN BOOKS

A Division of Penguin Books USA Inc.
375 Hudson Street, New York, New York 10014
Penguin Books Ltd, 27 Wrights Lane, London W8 5TZ (Publishing & Editorial) and
Harmondsworth, Middlesex, England (Distribution & Warehouse)
Penguin Books Australia Ltd, Ringwood, Victoria, Australia
Penguin Books Canada Ltd, 10 Alcorn Avenue, Toronto, Ontario, Canada M4V 3B2
Penguin Books (N.Z.) Ltd, 182–190 Wairau Road, Auckland 10, New Zealand

First published by The Viking Press 1972
Published in Puffin Books 1982
10   9   8
Copyright © 1972 by Betsy Byars
All rights reserved

Library of Congress Cataloging in Publication Data
Byars, Betsy Cromer.   The house of wings.
Reprint. Originally published: New York: Viking Press, 1972.
Summary: Left with his grandfather until his
parents are settled in Detroit, Sammy learns to
respect and love the old man as they care for an
injured crane together.
[1. Cranes (Birds)—Fiction. 2. Grandparents—Fiction]
I. Schwartz, Daniel, 1929–    , ill. II. Title.
PZ7.B9836Ho 1982   [Fic]   82-607 ISBN 0-14-031523-3  AACR2

Printed in the United States of America

# CONTENTS

## WILDERNESS HOUSE

Sammy crouched in the metal culvert that ran beneath the highway. His head was bent forward over his dusty knees. His shoulders were hunched, his eyes shut. He was listening.

At first there was only the sound of his own ragged breathing and the hum of cars on the highway above. Then he heard it.

"Boy!"

Sammy's head snapped up. He stared at the circle of light at the end of the culvert. He waited. His face was dusty and, beneath the dust, red. Tears had washed the dust away in streaks down the sides of his cheeks. He had cried so hard that he had gotten the hiccups.

"Boy, where are you?" his grandfather called. "Boy!"

Sammy did not answer. He remained bent over in the position of a runner about to start a race. One hand, still wet with tears, was braced on his knee; the other hung at his side. His fingers nervously pinched up the pale sand in the bottom of the culvert and released it.

"Boy, are you in that pipe? You hear me?" His grandfather's voice was louder and Sammy knew he was close, probably climbing up the bank right now. "Do you hear me?"

Sammy ran in a crouch through the pipe. He came out the other side in the grass divide between the highways and waited. He was bent over in a knot. He hiccuped loudly.

Someone threw an empty Fresca can from one of the passing cars, and it rolled down the bank. Sammy raised his head. He saw the cars flashing by and the sky beyond, which was the bright blue of construction paper.

He did not move. After a moment he leaned over and glanced through the pipe. At that exact moment his grandfather looked through the pipe on the other side and they saw each other. It was a strange sensation. It was as if they were the only two people in the world, staring at each other through the center of the earth.

Neither of them spoke. Sammy was silent because the sight of his grandfather made him sick with anger. His grandfather was too winded to speak. His grandfather was holding on to the top of the pipe with one hand and holding his side with the other. His chest and shoulders were rising and falling rapidly.

The silence was broken as Sammy hiccuped. Then his grandfather said through the pipe, "Listen, boy, your mom and dad didn't leave you because they wanted to." Through the culvert, his voice had a deep ringing sound. It was as unreal as what he was saying.

Sammy pulled his lips back in a snarl. "Liar!" he shouted. "Liar!"

His grandfather had his mouth open to speak again, but he closed it when Sammy said this. He looked down at his feet. He was still holding on to the top of the pipe, breathing hard. When the word *liar* had stopped washing over him, he looked up and said, "They had to get on their way, boy. That was why they didn't wait to tell—"

"I don't want to hear about it," Sammy shouted.

"They wanted me to—"

"I don't want to hear, I don't want to hear, I don't want to *hear*. Can't you understand English?"

He turned and ran across the grass median to the pipe that went under the other half of the highway. In a crouch he ran through the pipe, came out on the run, and kept going.

He did not have any idea where he was now or where he was heading. He had found the pipe by chance, and he would find another hiding place and then another. "And don't you follow me either," he shouted over his shoulder, even though his grandfather was nowhere in sight.

Sammy ran to a small grove of trees and paused to look back. He waited. There was a silence broken only by the faint sound of the leaves overhead being turned by the wind. He hiccuped. He leaned against one of the trees, putting his arm tiredly around it as if it were a friend. His eyes kept watching the dark hole of the culvert.

After a minute he saw his grandfather emerging from the pipe, tumbling out like an unwieldy crab. His grandfather straightened and looked up. He managed to look at the exact spot where Sammy was standing. "Boy!"

"Old man," Sammy called back.

"Wait for me, I'm—"

"Get away," Sammy hollered. "Let me alone!" He turned and started running again. "Dirty liar!"

His legs were heavy. His bare feet were sore. He was almost at the end of his strength and he knew it. The fact that the old man had somehow kept up with him enraged him and enabled him to run a little faster for a moment. Beneath his breath he muttered again and again, "Dirty liar."

He stumbled out of the trees and into an old cornfield. There was a wooden shack in the field, doorless and empty, leaning downhill. Sammy looked from the shack over to the thick woods. The woods would be a better hiding place but the shack was closer. He ran behind it, sank to the ground and leaned back against the warm, rough wood. In the distance he could hear his grandfather calling, "Boy, wait for me!" Sammy dropped his chin on his knees and did not answer.

He closed his eyes. For a moment he was dizzy, and he wrapped his fingers in the weeds and clung to keep from toppling over. He did not know what had happened to him. The hot sun and the running and the hard knot of pain in his chest made the whole thing seem like a fever dream.

It seemed to Sammy that his life had been, up until this morning, one long flowing time. For ten years he had been free. He had been part of the world the way a bird is or an animal. He had gone where he wanted and had done the things that pleased him. He had come home when he was ready to eat, and slept, if he liked, curled up on the sofa like a puppy. His parents had allowed him to raise himself because he was the last of eight children and they were worn out.

He had thought life would always be like that, with him just floating along and doing what he pleased. Now without warning, everything had changed. Like a fish, he had been thrown out of that warm current, and the change had been so sudden he could not understand it. He tried to go over the events in his mind.

Two days before, he and his parents had set out from Alabama in the truck. His father was going to get a job in Detroit, and the thought of a big city with new places to explore had pleased and excited Sammy. He had sat in the back of the truck, jammed between the boxes and belongings, shouting at the cars that passed, "We're going to Detroit." He had curled up and slept occasionally, but most of the time he had sat backward, waving at the people, saying to anyone who would look at him, "We're going to Detroit."

For two hot dusty days and one night they had driven, stopping to cool the engine and to let

13

Sammy's father lie by the truck and rest on a faded quilt with his hat over his face. Sammy had spent the rest time climbing people's fences, feeding weeds to strange sheep, wading in streams, running from place to place like a dog freed from his pen until his mom would call, "Sammy, come on now. We're leaving."

Late on the second day they had stopped in northern Ohio to spend the night with Sammy's grandfather. It was dark when they arrived. Sammy's mother had gotten them lost twice before they found the right road, and then the driveway had been so overgrown with weeds that they couldn't drive up to the house. Sammy's father had parked the truck back by the trees.

"You awake, Sammy?" His father had slapped his hand on the side of the truck and Sammy's eyes had opened.

"I'm awake," he said, but it was only partly true. Two days of being jiggled around in the back of the truck, baked by the sun and dried by the wind, had tired him. He climbed out of the truck stupidly. He stumbled in the dark and said, "Is this it?" He couldn't see anything but weeds and in the distance a big house that in the moonlight looked old and empty. "This can't be it."

His mother was not paying any attention to him. She was standing by the truck with her arms wrapped around her as if she were cold. She said, "Everything is so run down."

"Well, your dad's old now," his father said.

"But it used to be a real fine place. Ten years ago when we were here for Mamma's funeral, everything was real fine. Don't you remember?"

Sammy said, "I think this is the wrong house or something."

His father looked at his mother and said, "Well, your ma was the one who kept everything up. She was the—"

"It's like the wilderness," his mother said.

Sammy's grandfather came around the side of the house then. Sammy couldn't see him clearly. There was just the impression of a wild old man, blinded temporarily by the car lights.

"Who's there?" Sammy's grandfather asked. He lifted his arms to block out the lights.

"Papa, it's me," his mother said.

"Who?"

"*Me.*"

"Is it Judy?" His grandfather was coming slowly, squinting into the light.

"No, Papa, I'm Lucille." She stepped forward so

15

he could see her. "I'm Lucille and this is Harry and this is our boy Sammy. Sammy was just a baby when we were here last, so I guess you don't remember him."

His grandfather looked as if he didn't remember any of them. "Lucille?" he said in a confused voice.

"Yes, Lucille. There was Judy and Mary Louise and then me, Lucille."

His mother paused as if waiting for an invitation to come into the house. Sammy didn't wait. He started walking.

The house had looked dark, but as he got closer Sammy saw that there was a light in the hall. An old forty-watt bulb hung from the ceiling and gave off a faint glow.

Sammy went up the steps and crossed the sagging porch. The door was open and the light inside had drawn a moth. Sammy stopped at the door. There was a goose in the hallway and it did not move, just looked at Sammy with bright black eyes. Sammy stood tiredly, looking back at the goose, blinking with sleep. He yelled, "There's a goose in here, Mom!" No one answered him.

He took one step toward the goose and then he called out, "Where do I sleep?" He thought he would drop down in the hall. "Where do I sleep?" he called again.

"Just go on in the back room," his mom called. "Is that all right, Papa, if he sleeps in the back room?" Sammy couldn't hear his grandfather's reply, but his mom called, "Just go on in the back room, Sammy."

Sammy passed the goose with caution. He was not a polite boy, but he muttered "Excuse me" as he circled the goose and went to the back room. He fell across the bed and closed his eyes.

In the hall his mother was saying, "Papa, what are these geese doing in the house?"

Sammy heard his grandfather's slow answer, "Well, they just come in."

"Papa, if you'd have some screen put in the front door and keep it closed—"

"I don't mind them," his grandfather said. "They're company."

"But, Papa, you can't keep house if you've got geese tramping through." She broke off, then said louder, "Papa! What's happened to Grandma's portrait. It looks like birds have been roosting on it."

"A lady give me a canary," his grandfather mumbled.

"What?"

"A lady give me a canary," he said louder, "and for the first two months I had it, it wouldn't do nothing but walk across the top of that picture frame."

"Papa, you cannot keep house like this. It's disgraceful. What you have got to do is . . ." And in the middle of his mother's housekeeping advice, Sammy fell asleep.

He awoke once before daylight. He lay there for a moment, listening to the sound of the crickets. Then in a room above him he heard his mother. She was saying shrilly, "Harry, there's something flying in this room."

"It's just a bird. Go on back to sleep."

"Just a bird! Well, maybe you can sleep with birds flying all over, but I can't. What's going on in this house anyway?"

"Go to sleep."

"Harry, it's an *owl*. Listen."

"Go to sleep."

"Harry, it went in the closet. If you get up and close the door before it flies out . . ." There was a pause. Sammy could hear his father's feet on the floor. Then his mother snapped angrily, "Now it's loose again and it's going to be bothering us all night. You know how owls are."

Sammy turned over and fell asleep waiting to hear if his father was going to do anything about the owl. When he awoke for the second time it was ten o'clock in the morning. He lay on the bed without moving for a moment. The only thought in his mind was that he was hungry. The afternoon before he had had a Moon Pie and an R C Cola when they stopped at a gas station, and he had not eaten since.

Slowly he got out of bed and stood on the floor. His feet could feel the grit on the bare boards; it was as fine as spilled sugar. In the dusty discolored mirror over the dresser he could see himself. He looked strange, and suddenly that was the way he felt too.

He turned and walked out into the hall. His red hair was standing up like a rooster's comb. He said, "Mom!"

The floor in the hall was so dirty that it appeared to be a continuation of the yard. Mud had been tracked in and had dried, so that there were ridges in the dirt like corduroy. Sammy looked into the parlor. Curtains hung at two of the windows; the others were bare. The furniture was old and faded. One of the legs of the sofa was broken off and had been replaced by a concrete block.

Sammy stood in the hallway without moving. He had been to this house only once, when he was

19

a baby, and he did not remember it. He had heard his older brothers talk about his grandfather's house, though, and a picture had formed in his mind. The picture was of a large white house set in a green meadow.

His brother Tom had told him of croquet games on the front yard and lemonade stands at the end of the driveway. According to Tom, a person could make a living doing nothing but selling lemonade on that road.

Jim had told him about a peacock who strutted up and down the drive and opened up his feathers like a fan whenever Aunt Minnie came out in the yard. The peacock was the only admirer Aunt Minnie ever had.

And Bertie had told him about his grandfather's parrot, who had once belonged to a man with a gas station, and this parrot could say anything that had to do with cars. It was a lot of fun, Bertie said, to take an unsuspecting person into the dining room and ask the parrot, "What's wrong with him?" because the parrot would say instantly, "Out of gas" or "Needs a muffler" or any of a dozen funny things. Sammy had decided that the first thing he would do when he got to his grandfather's was to run into the dining room and listen to the parrot talk about cars. "What's wrong with me?" he would ask.

Sammy walked back down the hall. He found the dining room and looked in, but there was no parrot. There was not even a place for a parrot, Sammy thought, only a dark dusty table, seven empty chairs, and a cabinet without any china left in it. He wondered if there had ever been a parrot, or a peacock on the lawn. His mom had been right. This was the wilderness.

He walked out onto the porch, shielding his eyes from the hot sun. "Mom!" He did not see anybody. He went down the steps, taking them one at a time because the steps sagged on one side. There was a large hole worn into the earth at the bottom of the steps, and a rock had been set to fill it. Sammy stood on the warm rock, curling his toes over the edge. He looked out over the yard. For the first time he began to feel alarmed. He didn't see the truck.

"Mom!"

He left the rock and walked quickly through the weeds. Then he started running. He ran to the trees where the truck had been parked.

He stood there a moment, looking at the imprint of the tires in the weeds. He could see where the truck had stopped. He walked slowly forward and paused. He could see where the truck had turned around and then he could see where the truck had left. It was as plain as railroad tracks.

He heard a shuffling noise behind him and he spun around, startled. He saw his grandfather. His grandfather looked wild even in the daylight. He wore an old railroad man's jacket and faded soldier's pants and a cowboy's shirt and miner's boots. Sammy didn't think his grandfather had been any of those things.

Sammy stood where he was in the tracks of his father's truck. He watched his grandfather. There was no sign of greeting in Sammy's face.

His grandfather crossed the yard slowly, shuffling along in the weeds. The miner's boots were too narrow, and he had cut out the sides.

Sammy said, "Where's my mom and dad?" He spat out the words. It was an accusation. "What'd you do with them?"

His grandfather cleared his throat. His army pants were big and loose because he had sewn some extra cloth in each side. He had his hands hooked into the belt loops. He cleared his throat again and wiped either side of his mustache with his hand. His skin had the soft dustiness of leather.

"Where's my mom and dad?" Sammy asked again. His voice rose because he suddenly knew that they had not merely gone into town or to the gas station. He reached out and grabbed the front of the railroad jacket and shook his grandfather. "Where's my mom and dad?" His grandfather rocked slowly back and forth like a buoy in the water.

Then his grandfather said one word. "Gone." It was like the sound of an old sad church bell in the hot empty yard. "Gone."

## RUNNING AWAY

Sammy could not believe he had heard correctly. He released his grandfather's jacket and stepped back as if to improve his hearing. He dared his grandfather with his eyes. He said, "What did you say?"

His grandfather held out one hand. "They're gone," he said. "Your mom and dad is gone."

"What are you talking about?" Sammy was small and he had the wariness and quickness of an animal. Now his eyes narrowed and he came forward one threatening step.

His grandfather was still holding out his hand. It was trembling a little with uncertainty and age. "This morning," he said, "when your mom and dad got up, they was talking about all the trouble they was going to have getting settled in Detroit.

Your dad doesn't have a job yet, boy. They may even have to sleep in the truck. Well, then, while we was talking, it just came about naturally that you would be better off staying here with me."

"They wouldn't leave me like that."

"They didn't want to wake you. It was—"

"They wouldn't."

"Listen, I tried to tell them," the grandfather explained. "I said, 'You better *tell* the boy, hadn't you, before you go driving off?' But your ma said you'd make a fuss. She said once you saw they was gone you'd be fine. She said that's the way you always were. She—"

"Liar!"

The grandfather stepped back. He began to rub his hands together. He said, "Listen, boy, they're going to send for you. In August they're going to write me a post card and I'm going to take you in to Gatsburg and put you on the bus. It's not—"

"Where did they go? Don't you lie to me!" Sammy's hands had become fists, hard as rocks.

"They went on to Detroit," his grandfather said. "That's all that's happened. They went on *first*." He nodded. "You and me, boy, can—"

"What *really* happened?"

"They went on to Detroit," the grandfather said

in his same patient voice. Then, fumbling a little, he put out his hands and tried to take Sammy by the shoulders. "Boy—"

Quickly Sammy stepped back. He looked at the outstretched hands with the suspicion he would give a steel trap. Then he looked at his grandfather's face. His own face drew into a sneer.

"Liar!" he said. "Dirty, stinking liar. They wouldn't leave me." He spun around in the weeds. "Liar, liar, *liar!*" And then he started running.

He ran between the tracks of his father's truck. He ran hard and fast, his arms pumping machine-like at his sides. He was going so fast that when he came to a stop on the pavement of the road he burned his feet. He glanced over his shoulder. "Liar!" he cried to the trees.

He hesitated. He had been sleeping in the back of the truck when they had turned off the road the night before, and he was not sure now which direction to take. He heard his grandfather shuffling through the weeds behind him. Quickly Sammy turned to the right and started running along the white center line of the road.

"Boy! Wait, boy!" his grandfather was crying behind him. "Boy, you're going to get to ride on the bus to Detroit. You're going to Detroit on the—"

"Shut up," Sammy shouted."And I'm not waiting for any bus either."

"Boy!" It was like a last gasp. Sammy kept running. He thought with satisfaction that if he turned now, he would see his grandfather standing helplessly in the weeds on the side of the road. His old shoulders would be sagging with defeat. Sammy decided that was something he wanted to see, and he turned around without breaking his stride. Instead he saw that his grandfather had turned onto the road and was running behind him. He was slow and heavy but he was coming.

His grandfather saw him look back and he cried, "Boy!" He put out one hand.

"Old man," Sammy shouted back, sneering. Then he looked ahead and concentrated on his running.

There was not a car on the road, and the asphalt was hot under Sammy's bare feet. Ahead of him the heat was causing the road to disappear. Suddenly as he ran he began to feel strange and lightheaded.

"Boy!"

Sammy kept running. He had always been a good runner, but today something was wrong. It was the sun or the hunger or maybe it was the hard knot that had come in his chest when his grandfather had said "Gone." He had not run far at all, only past the first bend in the road, when he began to feel tired. His eyes stung. His legs hurt. He wanted to lie in the shade by the road and rest. He wanted to put wet leaves on his eyes. He forced himself to keep going. When he was a hundred miles up the road, he decided, *then* he would stop. It was even possible, he told himself, that he could overtake his parents. If the truck overheated again, he might come upon them beside the road, his father asleep on the quilt. He thought of flinging himself down on his father's chest. He thought of his father lifting his hat from his face and saying in a pleased voice, "Well, where'd you come from?" The hard knot moved up into his throat.

He could hear his grandfather behind him, gasping out from time to time the word "Boy!" He could hear the heavy shuffling of his grandfather's feet. "Boy!" He did not look around, but it seemed to him that perhaps his grandfather was slowing down. His voice was getting weaker anyway.

Sammy was getting weaker too. He stumbled, went down on one knee, and got quickly to his feet. Blood began to trickle down his leg. He did not even notice. He glanced over his shoulder and gasped to his grandfather, who was too far away to hear, "I didn't hurt myself." He kept running and after a while he stumbled again.

As he rounded another turn he saw the super-highway ahead. On the grassy bank leading up to the highway was a culvert. Sammy ran slower, then he hesitated and stopped. Glancing back to make sure his grandfather couldn't see him, he jumped across the drainage ditch, scrambled up the bank, and crawled into the pipe.

Halfway through the pipe he decided he was safe. His grandfather would never think to look for him in here. His grandfather would run on down the road, thinking he was getting farther and farther behind. Finally his grandfather would have to turn around and go home.

Sammy sank down in the culvert and let his face drop into his hands. The knot in his throat was choking him. He could not swallow. He could not even breathe. There was a moment in which this pain in his throat was so great he could not even move.

Then, abruptly, he began to sob in a wild, tearless way. He did everything but shed tears. He kicked and shook his fists. He punched at the air. He made choking strangling noises in his throat. He cursed. He socked his head. He struck the pipe until his hands were bruised. He wailed, throwing himself around in the culvert like a fish out of water.

And then he put his head on his arm and didn't move at all. The tears came then, hot tears that burned his eyes. They rolled off his face and onto his arm and left a strangely cool, wet track behind.

Sammy was lying there, completely spent, when he heard his grandfather's voice. He got up in a crouch and listened. Then in a few minutes his grandfather had appeared, and the chase had begun all over again, through the culverts, across the field.

That was what had happened, and now Sammy sat behind the old shed, wondering about it, going over it in his mind. He felt he could sit here all day thinking about it and never understand. His life had changed and it was never going to be the same again. That was the only thing that was certain, that and the fact that his grandfather was to blame.

Dully Sammy looked around. There were woods to the right, and up the hill beyond the old cornfield, the brush thickened and there were clumps of rocks and small trees. It seemed to Sammy suddenly that he had chosen the poorest hiding place of all.

"Boy!"

Sammy got to his feet. He peered around the side of the shed. His grandfather was coming up the hill toward him. He felt trapped.

"Boy!"

# A CRY IN THE FOREST

Sammy hesitated and then he stepped out from behind the shed so that his grandfather could see him. He glared down the hill. He hated his grandfather with a fierceness that made him shudder. He wanted to pick up one of the boulders by the shed and throw it down the hill. He wanted his grandfather to hear the sound of the boulder coming toward him, rumbling and threatening, and know that Sammy hated him that much.

Sammy shouted, "You better let me alone!" His voice seemed thin and sad in his ears. It was not at all the thundering demand he had intended. He said it again, screamed it. "Let me alone!" His throat began to hurt.

His grandfather looked up. He did not answer. He just kept coming up the hill with one slow steady step after another.

Sammy said, "Don't you ever get tired?" He threw the words down the hill at his grandfather. He thought his own legs were going to collapse at any moment, and he wondered how this old man could keep going on and on.

His grandfather stopped for a moment. He looked down at his feet in the open-sided miner's boots. He bent and pulled a stick out of the side of his shoe, then he straightened. He held on to a small tree like it was a staff. He said, "I get tired like everybody else."

"Then let me alone. I don't want you following me. You ain't got any right."

His grandfather looked back down at his feet, as if he was thinking over the matter. Then he ducked his head and started coming up the hill again. Sammy felt tears in his eyes. As he spun around and started running, they sprayed out onto his face.

He left the shelter of the shed and ran up the hill. Halfway to the top he stumbled, went down on one knee, and stopped. He rested and then got up and turned around. He said, "You'll never catch me. Never!"

He staggered to the top of the hill, turned around, and stood there for a moment. The colors began to blur. The weeds and brush, the old cornfield, the forest all ran together. He blinked his eyes. He meant to stand there just long enough for his grandfather to get one last look at him. Then he planned to run down the other side of the hill and be gone forever.

Sammy waited. He had lost sight of his grandfather. He thought maybe he was behind the shed, resting in secret, so Sammy remained where he was, legs planted apart. Then he called, "You'll never see me again. Did you hear that?"

Still there was no sign of his grandfather. Sammy glanced over his shoulder. The other side of the hill sloped to a stream, and Sammy decided he would stop there long enough to get a cool drink and soak his feet. Then he would go. Quickly he turned back to see if his grandfather was in sight yet. He was not.

Sammy looked around uneasily. He thought suddenly that there might be some trick involved in the disappearance of his grandfather. He thought perhaps his grandfather was creeping up through the forest, circling behind him, planning to catch him unaware.

There were some rocks to the right and Sammy went over and crouched behind them. He waited. There was not a sound anywhere. Leaning on one

34

knee, he glanced around the largest rock. His grandfather was still not in sight.

Suddenly Sammy wanted very much to know where his grandfather was. He began to glance around. Suspiciously, he watched the trees, the shed, the brush for any sign of movement. His grandfather could be crawling up the hill on his belly like a snake for all Sammy knew.

Two white butterflies were fluttering over Sammy's head, and he hit at them and hissed, "Get away, you!" They flew in a small circle as if caught in a miniature tornado. "Get away!" He thought that all his grandfather would have to do would be to look up and see the two butterflies. Then he would come running up the hill. "Aha!" And there Sammy would be, squatting under the butterflies, scowling. He hit at the butterflies again. "Get away."

Suddenly there was a noise in the trees just down the hill. It was a shrill trumpeting cry. Sammy thought of a wild goose, but he knew it could not have been that. The noise was too loud. He waited, bent over behind the rock. The sun on his back was hot. The weeds scratched his legs. The butterflies moved away unnoticed, still going around in a small circle.

35

Sammy waited a moment longer. Then he stood up and looked directly down the hill, not worrying now about his grandfather seeing him. He was puzzled. As he stood there the sound came again from the woods. It rolled through the air, and then Sammy heard the sound of someone running.

Sammy hesitated. He did not know what to do. He began to walk slowly down the hill and toward the woods. When he was in the shade he stopped and stood behind a tree.

He waited motionless in the shadows. Then he heard his grandfather's cry. "Boy!" His grandfather's voice was so high with excitement that Sammy almost did not recognize it.

He did not answer because he thought again it was a trick. If he went running down the hill, drawn by curiosity, then at some point his grandfather would pounce out from a hiding place and cry, "Got you!" Sammy used to catch an old cat named Albert that way, so he knew the trick well.

He heard the strange trumpeting sound again. And then his grandfather called, "Boy, quick! Come here if you want to see something."

That was the oldest trick in the world. More suspicious than ever, Sammy glanced over his shoulder at the top of the hill. He thought about the stream, and he was tempted to start the long journey to Detroit right then. Still, there had been something in his grandfather's voice that stopped him. Slowly he started walking down the hill. Anyway, he thought, if it is a trick I can always get away later.

Kicking at the weeds, he walked toward his grandfather's voice. "Boy!" Sammy hesitated. Then he answered with a sigh, "I'm coming."

"Over here."

Sammy started loping along. He began to run. He called, "Where are you?"

"Over here. *Here.*"

Sammy went into the woods. He began to move with more caution now because a trick would be easier here. He stopped altogether after a moment and said, "I don't see you." He glanced around quickly. He could almost feel his grandfather's grip, hear the triumphant, "Got you!" He tried to look in every direction at once.

"Over here!" His grandfather had lowered his voice to a hush now, and this gave it a new urgency.

"I'm coming as fast as I can." Sammy picked his way through the underbrush. He could see his grandfather's broad back ahead in the trees. There was something about the set of his body, the way he was standing perfectly still with one hand stretched to the side like a patrol guard, that made Sammy move cautiously. His grandfather's bull neck was thrust forward. His whole body seemed to be leaning.

"What is it?" Sammy asked. His grandfather did not answer but continued to stand without moving. "What is it?" Sammy asked. "What's wrong?" He was uneasy and he hung back. There was something wild about his grandfather. Sammy said, "I'm not coming any farther until you tell me what it is."

With one hand his grandfather beckoned him forward. Sammy could see his grandfather's face now, sharp with intent. The thrust of his brow gave him the look of an old lion made young by the excitement of the hunt.

Sammy took another step. He hesitated. His eyes tried to look through his grandfather and see what was holding him.

"Look," his grandfather said. He jabbed at the air with his outstretched hand.

Sammy kept taking one slow step after another. He was almost by his grandfather's side before he saw what his grandfather was seeing. Then he stopped and let his breath out in a long low whistle.

# GIT!

*A*gainst the brush in the slight clearing ahead stood the biggest bird Sammy had ever seen. It was over three feet tall with long stiltlike legs, awkward body, curved neck. Its feathers appeared to be gray, the wings and back washed with brown, and there was a bald red crest on top of its head. The bird was ruffled and dirty as if it had been battered about, but it still had the bearing of a warrior.

"What is it?" Sammy asked. He tried to move closer but his grandfather put out one arm and held him back. Sammy could easily have ducked under his grandfather's arm; he had done that dozens of times at parades and crowds, but for some reason he remained where he was. Without looking up at his grandfather, he said again, "What is it?"

"Crane," his grandfather said.

39

Sammy had never seen such a bird. He had never heard of one either, and he did not trust his grandfather's knowledge. "A what?" he asked. A faintly scornful smile pulled down the corners of his mouth.

"A crane."

Sammy was awed by the size of the bird and by the way it stood, its head held high on its long neck. He did not speak for a moment. Then he shook his head and said stubbornly, "It don't look like any crane I ever saw."

The crane took one step to the right, and Sammy saw that its left wing was hanging lower than the other. The S-shaped neck straightened as the crane raised its head.

His grandfather said, "Yes, it's a crane all right."

"When did you ever see a crane before anyway?" Sammy asked.

His grandfather lowered his arm as he thought. "Last crane I seen was in Florida, I reckon, when I was a boy. A man down the road from us had four of them—they were like pets. And I remember that one of them cranes used to come around the neighborhood during horsefly season, and that crane would stand at the door and call out—kind of a chirping noise—and people would open up their front doors, and this crane would come right on in the house and eat the horseflies off the screens. I wasn't any bigger than you when that happened, only I never have forgotten it."

Sammy was listening to his grandfather so intently that his mouth was hanging open. "Is that the truth?" he asked. Then, as if he had been caught off guard, he wet his lips and with a touch of scorn said, "That don't sound like any crane I ever knew."

Sammy's grandfather's hearing was good, but people thought it wasn't, because he didn't pay attention to anything he didn't want to hear. He continued now as if Sammy had not spoken. "And that crane knew which people would let him in and which people wouldn't, and he would only go to the houses that wanted him."

"Did he come into your house?" Sammy asked.

"We was always glad to see him, as I remember it. We welcomed him. We kept pigs and cows then and the flies would get fierce." His grandfather had not looked at Sammy while he was talking, just kept watching the crane, and he was speaking in such a soft easy way that the crane was still standing there. "That crane I'm speaking of lived to be twenty-one years of age."

"Twenty-one?"

"Yes, twenty-one."

"I never heard of any crane getting to be twenty-one," Sammy said. His grandfather shifted his weight but did not move toward the crane. "Fourteen maybe, or fifteen," Sammy added, yielding a little on this one point, "but no crane that I knew ever got to be—"

His grandfather took a step forward while Sammy was speaking, and a dry stick cracked beneath his foot. Abruptly the crane moved to the side. He walked with quick, jerking steps, and his head moved forward, held a little to the left. Then the crane turned his head around as if he were peering to see what had caused the noise. He hesitated. His head snapped higher. Then he began preening the feathers of his wing and back. He ran the feathers between his beak again and again in a quick nervous movement.

"What's he doing that for?" Sammy asked.

"He's trying to decide whether to run or fight. He's scared." Sammy's grandfather was standing with one foot ahead of the other, waiting for the crane to settle down. "Some birds do like this—act funny when they get scared. You ever had a rooster?"

"No," Sammy said. He added quickly, "I *could* have had one if I'd wanted it but—"

"If a rooster don't know what to do in a bad situation—say, a strange animal shows up—well, the rooster won't run, he'll start going through the motions of eating. There won't be a piece of food in sight and yet that old rooster will be pecking and eating as if his life depended on it. Some birds will start building a nest when they're upset. Some birds will go to sleep."

"If it was me I'd run."

Sammy's grandfather took a step forward. He said, "Just keep moving easy and talking quiet and don't startle him."

"Why don't he run *now*? You're getting closer and closer. He must know you're going to grab him."

"I don't know for sure. There's something wrong with him." He hesitated, then added, "Anyway I hope he don't run, because once he gets going he can outrun both of us, I can tell you that. My brother and I used to chase them cranes I was telling you about. We'd about kill ourselves running after them, and they would just keep striding along. They never even worked up a sweat." He resettled his hat on his head. He took another silent step. "Still," he added in a low voice, "there's something wrong here."

"What do you think it is?"

"I don't know yet. I'm going to catch him and maybe we'll find out."

"You going to eat him?" Sammy asked.

His grandfather turned around and looked at Sammy. His brows were pulled low. He said, "I'm going to catch him because he can't fly with that wing and it's just a matter of time till he dies out here in the woods."

"What could get him though? Foxes couldn't, or dogs. I bet nothing could. He could stab you all the way through the hand with that beak if he wanted to. Nothing could happen to that bird."

"He could starve to death or die of thirst. He could freeze if he lasts till winter." His grandfather was still looking at Sammy. "If he gets weak, anything roaming the woods could get him."

"Huh!" Sammy said. "I'd like to see that."

"Listen, boy—"

Sammy turned his head away with one sharp movement. When his grandfather called him "boy" the anger rose in him again. The memory of the chase washed over him. He looked down at the ground and then right into his grandfather's eyes. "Anyway, I don't care if he does die."

44    His grandfather seemed ready to add something

about the dangers of life in the woods, but he stopped. For the first time he looked as if he had been hit by what Sammy had said. "You what?"

"I don't care if he does die," Sammy repeated, glad to have hurt his grandfather at last. "He's nothing but a bird."

His grandfather looked hard at him. "I'll tell you something. Maybe you're not worth telling nothing to, but I'm telling you this anyway."

"You don't have to tell me nothing," Sammy said. "I'm not interested."

"When I was about your size, I was good at one thing and that was rock throwing. It was the only talent I ever had. I could throw a rock."

"Anybody can do that. That's nothing." They faced each other and glared.

"It was something, the way *I* done it," his grandfather said. "I could throw and I could *hit*. I could hit anything I could see. I'm telling you it was a *talent!*" Angrily he wiped the ends of his mustache. He glanced at the crane and then said in a lower voice, "Well, there was a redbird that roosted under the eaves of our house that particular year, and every day I would watch her. To get to her nest, this bird would have to hover beside it for a second. Well, one day I got a rock—I don't know to this day what made me do it—I got a rock and I waited by the corner of the house and when the bird came to her nest I aimed and I threw." He looked at Sammy. "And the bird fell down to the ground."

"You got it with just one rock?" Sammy had thrown hundreds of rocks at birds and never hit one.

"I hit it all right, hit and killed." His grandfather drew his heavy brows down low over his eyes.

"Killed it with one rock? It fell *dead?*"

"Well, it was fluttering its wings a little as I ran over, but by the time I got there it was dead." He wagged his head sadly. "I picked it up and I tell you, boy, I never felt any heavier weight than that dead bird. That bird was *something,* hear, and I didn't find it out until I was standing there with it dead in my hand. There's no such thing as 'nothing but a bird.' I learned that."

"Huh!"

"There ain't. You watch a bird in the air one minute, boy, and hold it lifeless in your hand the next, and you'll know what I'm talking about. And I learned doubly hard. Because then, to make up for what I'd done, I took them three baby birds and tried to raise them. Those birds were no more than three or four days old. All they could do was squirm and yawn. They couldn't even sit. You could still see the pink of their bodies."

"Did they live?"

"I thought they was going to at first. I took the nest in the house and I started feeding them grasshoppers. All day long my brother and me combed the fields for grasshoppers. Every fifteen minutes those birds wanted grasshoppers." He wiped his mustache. "Then one day one of the birds wouldn't open its eyes and it stopped begging for food and that afternoon it died."

"What about the others?"

"Well, one of them died too. I come in one morning and the nest was crawling with mites, and the birds, both of them, looked sick. I burned the nest and set the birds in a berry box, but one of them just got weaker and weaker and died. The last one lived to be set free, but I tell you one thing—I never threw a rock again."

When his grandfather finished Sammy straightened. He was disgusted with himself for listening, and this made his hatred for his grandfather sweep over him again. He jerked his head toward the crane. "Why should I care about a bird I never even saw before? He doesn't mean anything to me."

"I'm teliing you he should."

47

"And I'm telling *you* he don't!" Sammy's chin jutted forward and his head snapped up. The only thing that seemed different about them in that moment was that one was young and one was old. "I hope he *does* die."

His grandfather had an old dusty face and old dusty clothes, but his eyes, fixed on Sammy, were very bright. He said, "I don't reckon you mean that."

"I do too mean it. Let him die."

Behind his grandfather, the crane took one step toward the bushes. He tried to move through them, but the foliage was too thick. He remained pressed into the leaves.

"Boy, you don't—"

"Don't you tell me what I mean and what I don't mean! I wish that old crane would just fall down dead right this minute." Sammy glanced down, and his eyes focused on a rock by his foot. With his eyes blazing he picked up the rock and threw it at the crane. The rock missed, but the crane jerked his head around and tried to run forward into the bushes again.

Sammy's grandfather seemed to get a little taller. He said, "Well, you just go on to Detroit, hear? Just head on out of here. Keep on running as long as you want to. Ain't nobody going to try and stop you this time." He made a sharp shooing gesture with both hands. "Go on. You don't belong here."

Sammy stood there. He was startled by the violence of his grandfather's reaction. He stepped back and said, "I *will* go. You think I won't, but I will. I'll show you."

"Well, go on then. Show me. What are you waiting for?"

Sammy stuck out his chin and did not answer.

"Don't keep me standing here all day. I got work to do. I got to get this crane home one way or another. I got to save this crane's life. Get going!" His grandfather looked at him, his eyes burning in his old face. "What are you waiting for?"

"I'm not waiting for anything."

"Then go! Get away from here!" And then he spoke to Sammy as if he were an animal. "Git!" he said.

Sammy stayed as if he were rooted to the ground. His grandfather was wilder than his clothes now, wilder than the woods. He threw his hands into the air. "Git!" he cried again.

## DECISION

It would serve you right if I did go," Sammy said, baring his teeth. He continued to stand where he was. He put his hands on his hips and then he let them slide down into the pockets of his pants. He could feel his belongings—his knife, his fighting rocks, some rubber bands, a ring he had found on the road one day, a magnifying glass advertising Roger's Fertilizer, and some hazel nuts. They were things from home and Sammy felt surprised to find them there now. They were strange objects.

His grandfather was still staring at him. Sammy looked back at his grandfather, his chin out. In his pockets each of his hands clutched a rock. He kept these rocks in case of a fight. They fitted his hands perfectly. He could beat anybody with these rocks in his hands. He took his hands out of his pockets,

50

the rocks as tight in them as seeds in a peach, and put his fists up a little.

"Git!" his grandfather said. He was terrible to behold. He seemed to darken like a thunder cloud. His voice trembled with power. "Git!"

Sammy thought of a movie he had once seen on television. There was a huge statue towering over a tropical village and an earthquake had started. The huge statue had trembled and shaken and twisted, and then it had fallen forward, crushing the whole village and splitting the earth.

Sammy took one step backward. Still looking at his grandfather, he took another step. He kept doing this until he came up against a tree and then he stopped. He waited against the tree, the rocks getting a little looser in his hands.

He waited to see what his grandfather would say next, but his grandfather's face was set as firmly as if he would never speak again. His eyes were shadowed by his heavy brows so Sammy couldn't see what they were like, but he knew they were set and hard too.

There was a long moment in which Sammy and his grandfather looked at each other. Sammy said, "Why do you want me to go so bad anyway? You trying to get rid of me?" His voice had a strange sound. He clutched his rocks tighter again. "You can't make me go if I don't want to. Nobody can make me do anything!"

His grandfather kept looking at Sammy, but his face got softer. He lifted his shoulders a little and then turned away. He said, "Well, if you ain't going, then come on and help me with this crane."

Sammy hesitated. The desire to show his grandfather that he *would* go was strong, but the walk to Detroit seemed long and lonely. He was tired. The anger began to go out of him, not quickly, as it had his grandfather, but slowly, jerkily, bit by bit.

His grandfather was moving toward the crane as if he had already forgotten the trouble with Sammy. Sammy said to his back, "I didn't say I *wasn't* going." His grandfather did not answer and Sammy said, "It would serve you right if I did go. It would serve you right if I got lost and the police came." He said this in a lower tone of voice, mumbling the words, winding down. "Then you'd have some explaining to do."

"Hush up."

"Well, you would." He hesitated, then to add weight to what he had said, he added, "A boy I know got lost that way and they blamed it on the grandfather. They would even have put the grandfather in jail if the boy had wanted them to." The thought of his grandfather being led away to jail, the thought of saying generously, "Oh, let him go free," was comforting to Sammy.

"Hush up."

"It's true."

"Hush. It ain't."

"Well, it could be."

"If you're staying, hush." His grandfather smoothed his long, ragged mustache and turned away.

Sammy had the feeling that there was nothing he could say now that would get any reaction other than that absent-minded "Hush." He hesitated, then left the tree and started walking along behind his grandfather, shadow-like. As he walked, he put his fighting rocks back into his pockets.

The crane began preening his feathers again and then he stopped and lifted his head. There was blood on his breast, and Sammy said, "It looks like he's bleeding. See, right there." He pointed with one dirty finger to the line of stained feathers.

"He flew into something probably. It's unusual to see a crane around here, so something must have happened, something went wrong."

"What do you think?"

"Well, he could have been on his way north, to Michigan maybe, migrating, and got blown off course. We've had some bad storms this spring, one right after another. Then he could have got crippled flying into something and here he is." He shook his head. "I expect there's lots of birds that get lost migrating. Thirty sets out and only twenty-eight makes it."

The crane twisted his long neck around as they moved closer. Sammy's grandfather began to rub his hands together anxiously. He said, "I never caught a bird before in my life, not any kind of bird. I've had birds living with me the best part of my life, but I never went out and caught one."

"How did you get them though?"

"Did you see that owl in my house?"

"In your house back there?"

"Yeah."

"No, I didn't see any owl. He was flying in my mom's room though. She couldn't get to sleep because he was—"

"Well, I found that owl in my stove one morning."

"In your stove?" Sammy paused. "I never heard of any owl getting in a stove."

"Yes, in my stove. The owl got in the stove pipe

one night. The pipe was busted on top, and the owl probably fell out of the oak tree and just landed in the pipe and then tumbled on down into my stove. It was just a baby. Anyway, I was sitting there one night and I heard a plop. I didn't pay much attention to it, because I didn't hear anything more, just that one plop. It stayed in my mind though and the next morning I opened up my stove and there was the owl. He was covered with ashes, and I tell you he just looked as disgusted as anything. He looked like a mad old woman. Well, I took him out of the stove and fed him, and that's how I come to have an owl." He paused and looked again at the crane. "Only I never had to *catch* one." He kept rubbing his hands together.

"If it was me, I'd just rush up and grab."

"He ain't scared of us so maybe we can just ease up." His grandfather finished rubbing his hands and both of them looked at the crane.

The woods around them were quiet and it was beginning to get hot. Sammy felt lightheaded from hunger and the heat. His arms and legs were tingling. He suddenly thought that he would like to lie down in the shade and rest before doing anything about the crane.

He noticed that his grandfather, strong as an old    55

tree, was starting to move closer. Apparently his grandfather never got hot or tired or hungry. "Just don't make any sharp quick movements. That's the main thing," his grandfather said.

Sammy thought he could not make a sharp quick movement if his life depended on it. He said, "I'll try not to." He took another step along with his grandfather, putting his feet in his grandfather's footprints.

The leaves of the trees overhead began to move with a sudden breeze, but below, where Sammy was, the air was as hot and still as an attic. A gnat flew around his face and Sammy brushed it away.

His grandfather turned his grizzled face to Sammy. He said, "Well, we might as well do *something,* even if it's wrong. We can't count on him standing there forever."

"No," Sammy said.

His grandfather wiped his hands on his jacket. Sammy could see the intensity, the purpose in the set of his grandfather's shoulders, and he knew that if by some terrible chance the crane started to run away, his grandfather would run after him. His grandfather would run for the rest of this day and into the night if necessary. The crane would not get away. His grandfather could run for a week, a month, a year.

"Try to get him on the first grab," Sammy suggested. He thought that his grandfather would expect him to run along, to chase the crane until he dropped with fatigue. Sammy thought that would be about ten steps.

"I'll get him," his grandfather said, "one way or another."

And Sammy said tiredly to himself, "That's what I'm afraid of."

## THE CAPTURE

*H*is grandfather took another step toward the crane. Sammy went along, keeping right at his grandfather's elbow  The closer they got, the bigger the crane looked and the sharper the beak. Sammy said, "He sure is big for a crane." He looked up at his grandfather. "Wouldn't you say?"

His grandfather shook his head. "I seen a whooping crane at a zoo in Louisiana one time and it was about as tall as me. It would make two of that one."

"Yeah, but that was a whooping crane," Sammy said quickly. "This is big for a *regular* crane."

"A sandhill crane." His grandfather looked beyond the crane into the trees. He seemed to want to put off the actual capture of the crane as long as possible. He said, "I remember I got myself a bag of salted peanuts that day and the whooping crane came up to the wire fence and I threw him peanuts and he caught them in the air. A lady that was standing by told me that whooping crane would eat almost anything you threw him—hotdogs, hamburgers, french fries. Just toss it and he'd catch it. You don't see many of them whooping cranes any more."

He brought himself to the present with a start. Then slowly he began to take off his jacket. The railroad jacket was old, the lining was worn out, and the back of the jacket was so thin Sammy could see the sun shining through.

His grandfather shook out the jacket and held it up in front of him like an apron. His arms were thin and frail-looking compared to the rest of his body. They were as white as if they had never been exposed to the sun.

"What are you going to do?" Sammy asked.

"Well, I'm going to try to ease up on him and get this jacket over his head. There's something about not being able to see what's happening that calms a bird. A bird don't fight as much that way."

"Plus he won't be able to stab us with his beak."

"You just keep back while I'm doing this, only be ready to head him off if he starts running."

"I will."

His grandfather stepped forward. His foot rustled some dry leaves, and the crane's head snapped to attention. The crane stepped back against the bushes, pressing into the leaves in a quick startled movement. His head jerked around. His right eye, turned toward them, was a frosty yellow.

"He's making it easy for us so far," the grandfather said. "He's getting farther and farther back in the bushes. When I first seen him he was out there at the edge of the cornfield and he ran right in here like he didn't know where he was going. He trapped himself."

"He could still stab us though. His beak's longer than my knife."

"He can use it too. I've seen a crane stab that beak five inches into the ground and come up with a root."

His grandfather stepped closer. The crane moved with quick stiff steps against the brush without going anywhere.

"He's been in more trouble than we thought. Look, boy. His wingbones are rubbed raw, like he's been throwing himself up against something."

The crane did not move, but he was poised as if ready for the sound of a starting gun, ready for the race. He snapped his head up, listening.

The air in the forest was now charged with excitement. It was like the moment before a storm. Sammy forgot that he was hungry and tired, and he pressed closer to his grandfather. There was something about the bearing of the crane, the proud carriage despite his pitiful condition, that made Sammy want his grandfather to succeed.

"I'll take it from here," the grandfather said.

Sammy stepped back. He knew that the capture of the crane had begun, the stalk. Slowly his grandfather lifted his jacket, holding it against his side. Then he stepped forward in a slow careful way. The heavy miner's boots were soundless in the weeds.

Sammy waited. He swallowed and his throat was dust-dry. He blinked and his eyes seemed dry too, burned with the heat of the day and his excitement. Every muscle in his body was tight as a knot.

He kept his eyes on his grandfather as he moved toward the crane. His grandfather took three more steps without making a sound. The wind had died and silence hung over them like a tent.

"Be careful," Sammy said silently through his dry lips.

His grandfather took another step. Again Sammy heard nothing, but the crane jerked his head around

uneasily. He took a step forward with his long straight legs, moving around the bushes now, away from them. The crane took another step and paused.

Sammy and his grandfather waited. Sammy could see the air going out of his grandfather in a long silent sigh of relief when the crane did not run. If the crane stayed right where he was, Sammy thought, then the thick bushes would serve as a net, but if he moved . . .

His grandfather took a deep breath and stepped forward. The jacket was held loosely by his right side. With his left hand he pointed, directing Sammy, and slowly, carefully Sammy began to walk in the direction his grandfather had indicated, ready to head off the crane if he started to run.

Sammy picked his way noiselessly through the weeds. He looked down to see where he was stepping because the underbrush was thick here. Then he glanced up quickly to see if the crane had moved. He had not. The crane was still standing against the bushes, head high, turned away from them. Sammy's grandfather had not moved either. He was waiting, his body bent forward, the jacket half-raised.

Sammy took another step. He was watching the crane and this time his bare foot stepped directly on a long thorny vine. The thorns scraped his skin and he said "Ow" beneath his breath. As he raised his foot the vine wrapped around his ankle and the briers raked his skin. "Ow," he said, still talking only to himself. "Where are all these briers coming from?"

He took another step, avoiding the briers by stepping wide to the right. It was awkward and he paused to regain his balance before he proceeded.

He could see from the set of his grandfather's back that he was waiting impatiently for Sammy to get into position. Sammy took two quick steps forward. "I'm ready to head him off now," he said quietly. As he said this his foot landed on another thorn, and he jerked it up. In that instant he lost his balance. He took a heavy step to the right, landed on another brier, and pitched forward to the ground.

What happened next was so fast Sammy would have missed it if he had not snapped his head up as he fell. Startled by Sammy's fall, the crane wheeled around, headed directly into the bushes, then finding himself trapped, bounded out and threw himself forward. The crane started to run, moving in a frenzy, but Sammy's grandfather had come forward in one light fluid movement. It was such a quick reaction that he seemed for the moment to be a young man in an old disguise. He ran up and drew the jacket over the crane's head. It was as easy as covering a sleeping child. Then he pulled the jacket together at the crane's neck with his left hand and circled the crane around with his right.

He cried, "Got him!" holding the quivering crane and glancing at Sammy.

There was a flurry of movement from the crane, a series of hair-trigger reactions. The crane's good wing, which was pinned to his side, came free and beat at the air. Sammy's grandfather repinned the wing. The head and long neck twisted beneath the jacket. The grandfather loosened the cloth.

Then gently he lifted the bird against his side. The tips of his white elbows were as sharp as knives, and the crane's stick legs ran, scissors-like, in the air for a moment. It was a picture of sharp and impossible angles.

"Easy," his grandfather said. "Easy." There was another short struggle and then the crane was quiet. Sammy's grandfather looked at the crane and then at Sammy. "He's giving up now."

Sammy had risen to his feet during the struggle and now began mindlessly dusting off his pants. "Well, we got him," he said.

His grandfather's face was bright with success. His eyes were burning in his face. He held the crane against him like an enormous trophy. When he spoke his voice was still trembling with his excitement. "Yeah, we got him, boy," he said, generously including Sammy in the capture. "We got him."

## RAGGED WINGS

*S*till dusting off the back of his pants, Sammy came forward quickly and joined his grandfather. He looked at the crane's long stiff legs, now motionless. "Is he all right?"

His grandfather nodded.

"He looks dead."

"You feel his heart and you'll know he's not dead," he said. His hand was curled around the crane's chest and lay over the crane's heart. "A bird's got a big heart for his size. That's why he has to eat so much. Feel that." His grandfather was holding the crane awkwardly on his hip and he shifted a little.

Sammy reached out one dusty hand and touched the crane. The feathers of his breast were stained with blood. Sammy let his fingers rest there for only a second. He had not felt the heart at all but he said, "Yeah, he sure has got a big heart all right."

His grandfather said, "Now pull the bandanna out of my pocket and get it over his eyes instead of this jacket."

"Me?"

"Come *on,* boy."

Sammy hesitated. "Have any of these cranes ever attacked a person—anything like that?"

"I reckon so. One time my brother teased one of them cranes I was telling you about. He held out a piece of bread to the crane and then when the crane tried to take it my brother jerked it back. I tell you I never saw such a mad crane. His feathers rose and he spread his wings and he jumped on my brother and started beating him with his wings and stabbing him with his beak. Finally we had to just pull that crane off. It was something to see. My brother always claimed we took longer about it than we had to, but I tell you, a crane can get mad. There's no question about that."

"Oh."

"Now come *on,* boy. Get going."

"Well, where is the bandanna?" Sammy could see the bandanna in his grandfather's back pocket, but he didn't want to take it out. "I don't see any bandanna."

"In my pocket. Now get on with it."

Gingerly Sammy pulled the bandanna out of his grandfather's pocket. It was limp with grease and sweat, and Sammy stood holding it for a moment. "Now, what do I do? I've got the bandanna."

"Get it over his eyes."

"How?"

His grandfather sighed with disgust. "Just *do* it." Sammy lifted the side of the jacket. His grandfather shifted and said, "I've got his wings so you don't have to worry about them."

The wings weren't what Sammy was worrying about. Beneath the jacket the crane's head jerked. Sammy's heart was pounding in his throat. "I'm not going to do anything to you," he muttered. He got the bandanna ready. In the dusky warmth beneath the jacket the crane turned to Sammy. For a moment they were eye to eye. Sammy's hands started trembling. Then quickly, afraid to waste a moment, he covered the crane's head with the blindfold.

"Not too tight," his grandfather said.

"No." Sammy was weak with relief. With fingers that were still shaking he secured the bandanna and lifted off the jacket.

His grandfather checked it. "All right, let's go."

Sammy followed, holding his grandfather's

jacket. It was a strange procession as Sammy and his grandfather walked slowly out of the forest and across the old cornfield. "Here's the way I did it," Sammy said. Suddenly he wanted to tell about his success. "As soon as I saw the crane looking at me under the jacket, I knew I had to move fast. So I just very quickly and quietly slipped up with the bandanna, so—"

"I reckon that's what he's been eating," his grandfather interrupted as they crossed the cornfield. "Look close and you can see his bill marks in the ground around the stalks." Sammy glanced down. "This cornfield's been keeping him here."

"That and his wing," Sammy said. Sammy had been looking down to see the marks of the crane's bill in the ground and he bumped into his grandfather. He looked up.

Suddenly he was confused. It was not just the strangeness of the land. It was everything. It seemed to him a hundred years ago when he had been on the way to Detroit with his parents. A hundred years ago he had sat in the back of the truck and laughed and yelled, "We're going to Detroit."

"We're going to make this crane well," his grandfather was saying happily. "We'll get that wing bound up, get him fed."

"Won't he just go off when he gets well though?"

"Oh, sooner or later he'll go off." His grandfather was beginning to breathe heavily, but he kept talking. "I had me a blackbird once with a broken leg—a man brought it to me in an ice-cream carton. And I took care of that blackbird. I put a cast on its leg and I—"

"How could you make a cast for a bird?"

"Well, you get the leg straight and then you take a little plaster and dab it on and when it starts to harden you splint it with toothpick halves. Then you put on a little more plaster and wrap it with gauze. It makes a nice cast. When the leg's healed, you soak off the cast with vinegar. Anyway, getting back to what I was saying, that blackbird stayed with me all that fall and all that winter. He got attached to me. That happens with birds more than you'd think. He went everywhere with me, rode around on my shoulder."

"That doesn't sound like any blackbird I ever heard of before, riding around on somebody's shoulder."

"Well, that's what this one done. One time I walked into Gatsburg with that blackbird on my shoulder and a man took a picture of me and put it in the newspaper, in the *Gatsburg Press*."

71

Sammy stumbled a little looking up at his grandfather. His grandfather said, "Watch where you're going now, boy."

"I am watching, only what's this about the blackbird?"

"Well, that's all. They just put my picture in the newspaper. It made me famous. Kids would stop me on the street and ask, 'Where's your crow?' Kids called me the crow-man."

"I wouldn't mind having a blackbird like that," Sammy said. "Alabama blackbirds are more trouble than anything. They steal corn and—"

"A blackbird makes a nice pet," his grandfather interrupted. "I guess a blackbird makes about the nicest pet there is. If you're eating, he comes over and helps himself right off your plate. If you're reading a magazine, he turns the pages for you. He unties shoelaces and opens packages. There wasn't nothing he couldn't do."

"This one blackbird did all that?"

"And if I put a toothpick in my mouth he'd come and have a game of tug of war."

"Have you still got him?"

"No, the blackbird's gone. He went off in the fall of last year. October 6."

"He just flew away without any warning?"

"Oh, no. He'd been flying free all summer, but he'd be gone for a few days and then come home. Then the last time I seen him was in October, October 6. He came up to the house in the morning and flew to his favorite perch outside the kitchen window. I opened the window and he hopped on my hand and I brought him in. We sat down at the table and had breakfast—he ate a piece of banana and some Wheaties and drank at the sink. Then he flew back out the window and was gone, heading south. I figured later it was migrating day."

"And you never saw him again?"

His grandfather shook his head. "I looked for him last spring but he never came."

"He could still come though, couldn't he?"

His grandfather didn't answer. He said, "The blackbird's gone. A canary a lady gave me is gone. My gray parrot's gone. My wild ducks are gone. The redbird. The thrashers." He began to tick off his losses in a slow sad voice.

"But you've still got the owl."

"One day the owl will go too. I don't keep the front door shut all the time, and one day he'll fly out and be gone."

"You could start shutting the door again, being real careful."

73

"I'll tell you something," his grandfather continued. "Every one of them birds that stayed with me is more real to me than the people I've known."

"Even your family?"

"I can't even get some of my own children straight in my mind, if you want the truth. I never have been able to tell the girls one from the other, and I got a son living in Louisiana that I wouldn't know if he jumped out from behind that bush yonder." He shook his head. "But, boy, I'll tell you something. I could pick my owl and my blackbird and my gray parrot and my canary and my wild ducks out of a thousand." He paused, breathing heavily. "I don't know why that is."

Sammy said, "I'm that way about a dog I had one time. I didn't have him but two weeks, but I'd know him anywhere. His name was Freckles."

"If that blackbird come flying over our heads right now, I'd know him."

"Same with my dog."

Sammy watched the crane for a moment. He was not moving at all now. The long serpentine neck was arched downward. Only a faint quiver from time to time showed he was still alive. Then Sammy looked up and saw the highway ahead, the culvert they would have to climb through.

"Let's hold on a minute," his grandfather said.

Sammy paused and glanced at his grandfather. Holding the crane against his side, the grandfather felt for his bandanna, realized it was over the crane's eyes, and mopped the back of his neck with his hand. Then he started walking again.

Sammy said, "The crane sure is quiet. It don't seem natural to me. If somebody was carrying me off with a blindfold over my eyes, I'd kick and holler and—"

"It's a funny thing with birds, with animals too. When you capture a wild bird or animal, well, a certain number of them will just die. I reckon it's the shock of the thing."

"You don't think the crane's dying, do you?" Sammy asked quickly.

"No, but I am thinking we ought to get him home as fast as we can."

"Yeah," Sammy said, "that's what I was thinking too."

## THE LONG WALK

As they walked toward the superhighway, both of them kept their eyes on the round circle of the culvert. Finally as they got closer, his grandfather cleared his throat and said what they were both thinking. "The hard part is going to be getting him through that pipe."

They paused at the foot of the bank. There was a concrete runoff leading down the bank and Sammy put one foot on it and rested. He said, "I don't think we can do it."

"We got to."

"Can't we go around some other way?"

"Not less you want to walk the five miles to Gatsburg and the five miles back."

"Well, we could climb that fence, wait till the traffic dies down, and run across. I know I could."

He had been dodging Alabama traffic since he was four.

"The traffic don't die down on a highway like this. When the cars thin out, the trucks get thicker. Anyway, I don't want to take a chance with this crane."

Sammy nodded. Slowly he and his grandfather climbed up to the culvert and started through. Sammy ran ahead. Bent forward, straining with the awkward bundle, his grandfather staggered behind.

Sammy could hear his grandfather wheezing. His breathing was so magnified that the sound filled the pipe. Sammy wanted to suggest that he set the crane down for a minute and rest. He hesitated and his grandfather said, "Keep going!" as if he had read Sammy's mind.

They came out of the culvert and stood for a moment in the grassy divide between the highways. "Keep going," his grandfather said again. Sammy started through the culvert. He glanced back once over his shoulder. The crane was struggling again, but his grandfather held him firmly. His grandfather's face looked like something carved of stone. Nothing could stop him.

Without speaking they got to the road. There

was a car passing, and a boy stuck his head out the window and yelled, "Hey, what you got?"

Neither Sammy nor his grandfather answered. They glanced up at the car and then down in a single motion.

"What you *got?*" the boy in the car called again. He was leaning far out the window now, his hair blowing back over his face. "Make Daddy slow down," he said to his mother, and the car slowed. He yelled, "What you got?"

Sammy looked up again. He hesitated. Suddenly he had an important feeling. He imagined how he and his grandfather looked to the people in the car. He relented. "We caught a crane!"

"A what?"

"A *crane!*"

Sammy watched the car go around a bend in the road with a little smile on his face, then he said to his grandfather, "Now *he*'ll probably try to get *him* a crane."

"Well, you don't get one by wanting it, I can tell you that."

"I know. And you can't buy one, can you?"

"No."

"Not even in a pet shop."

"You and me is probably the only people in the

world right now with a crane like this." He began to whistle beneath his breath, cheerfully wheezing out, "I've Been Working on the Railroad."

They kept walking. Sammy was now trying to step on the soft patches of grass because his feet hurt. He thought there were probably blood blisters on the bottoms. He found a little puddle of mud in the ditch and stood in it.

"Yonder's the driveway to the house," his grandfather said over his shoulder. "It won't be long now. We can cut through here."

Sammy looked up and nodded. He stepped out of the ditch and started through the weeds. In a few minutes he could see the house.

The house had a deserted look to it. The porch sagged. The paint had been washed off by the rain and worn off by the wind. All the shutters were gone but one. Vines covered the north side of the porch, and the roof leaned under the extra weight. The only sign that anybody lived there was the geese who were now coming out from under the porch.

The geese stood together, their heads turned to Sammy and his grandfather. Then they broke into a run. They came straight across the yard, honking a greeting, their long necks outstretched, and then they slowed down by putting out their wings. Sammy could feel the wind against his legs.

"Well, here's the welcoming committee," his grandfather said to Sammy, then to the geese, "You get along now. I ain't got time for you."

Keeping together, the geese flocked around the grandfather's feet. One stretched out her neck and hissed at Sammy. Sammy said, "I'm afraid I'm going to step on them."

"Well, they shouldn't get underfoot like that." His grandfather was jovial. He scolded happily, "Get along now. Get along."

"What do they do if you step on them?" Sammy asked, putting his feet down carefully.

"Holler."

"Oh."

"Or bite."

"Oh." Sammy respected these geese. He had decided the first moment he saw them that he would never tease them or cause them trouble of any kind. He only wished there was some way to get this across to the geese. "Nice geese," he said. "Good girls." Stepping carefully around them, Sammy went up the rotten stairs and into the front hall.

"Through the kitchen," his grandfather said.

Sammy walked quickly into the kitchen, which

was cluttered with dishes and boxes and sacks and papers. It looked as though his grandfather lived in the kitchen. Sammy walked around the big faded armchair by the stove.

He hesitated, and his grandfather pushed past him and took the crane out onto the porch. Sammy followed. His grandfather's face was flushed with excitement. "Get the blindfold off."

Sammy reached out, loosened the knot, and drew off the blindfold in one quick motion. Then he stepped back against the wall. He remembered how the crane had attacked his grandfather's brother for just teasing him with a piece of bread.

His grandfather set the crane down and stepped back a little too. "There," he said.

Instantly the crane fell to the floor. He folded up, his legs sticking straight out in front of him like a little child.

"He can't stand up," Sammy said. He was astonished. He had expected the crane to come out fighting. He had expected himself to be the first target. "What's wrong with him?"

"He's weak, that's all. Get some water." His grandfather, reaching out for the crane, kicked a bucket toward Sammy at the same time.

Sammy took the bucket and went quickly into 81

the kitchen. The pipes were so old that only a trickle of water came out of the faucet. Impatiently he twisted the handles.

"Hurry up," his grandfather called.

The bucket was only half full but Sammy took it to the porch. "If there was enough water in these pipes," he grumbled, "I would have—"

"There's nothing wrong with him," his grandfather said. He was on his knees beside the crane. "He's just weak. Give me the water." He grabbed the bucket from Sammy and held it beneath the crane's head. The crane took no notice of it.

Sammy's grandfather splashed some water on the crane's face. Then he dipped his beak down into the water. "There's nothing wrong with him. He's just weak."

"It looks like more than weakness to me," Sammy said.

"No," his grandfather said stubbornly, "he'll be all right in a minute." He dipped the crane's head into the water and this time the crane began to drink. He stuck his long beak into the water almost to the nostrils and then lifted his head and swallowed.

"That's all that was wrong," his grandfather cried. "He was just thirsty. See, boy, didn't I tell you?" The crane drank again. "I told you."

Still his grandfather looked worried, Sammy thought. His heavy brows were drawn together. The wrinkles in his forehead were so deep they could have been cut with a knife. Sammy said, "Yeah, he was just thirsty," but he turned his eyes away and stuck his hands in his pockets.

## DARK DISCOVERY

When the crane had finished drinking, Sammy's grandfather carried him out to the fenced field behind the house. Sammy ran along trying to help, but his grandfather said, "I've got him. You just get the gate." He sighed. "I bet this crane don't weigh ten pounds. He's like a sack of feathers."

Sammy ran ahead. Weeds had grown up in front of the gate and it was difficult to open. Sammy tugged at it and then yanked angrily. "What's wrong with this old gate anyway?" He wasn't sure whether it was the gate or his weakened arms.

"Lift it up."

Sammy tried to lift the gate, and then dragged it open, scraping it over the weeds. "I'm getting it," he said, yanking it inch by inch, "only this doesn't seem to be much of a place to keep a crane to me."

"It's shady and it's cool. It'll do."

The geese had followed the procession through the house and were now standing around the grandfather's feet, making cackling noises. One stuck out her neck and hissed at Sammy. Sammy said, "Don't these geese ever stay out of the way?"

"No." His grandfather was holding the crane out in front of him, waiting.

"All right, the gate's open, enough anyway," Sammy said. "If these geese would just stay out of my way, I could . . ." Sammy's voice trailed off as his grandfather walked over and went through the gate.

"What we got to do first," he said, "is get some food for him. I don't reckon he's had much from the look of him."

"When do *people* eat around here?" Sammy asked pointedly.

His grandfather set the crane down and then stepped back. "See, he's getting his strength. He's standing."

"Yeah, *he's* standing," Sammy said. He looked up at the sky, saw where the sun was, and knew he had missed both breakfast and lunch. For some reason he thought about a commercial he had seen on TV one time where little round pieces of cereal

85

danced in a chorus line. Those round pieces of cereal swam before his eyes.

"Go get the water," his grandfather said, "and get some of that corn in a sack by the door. Hurry now."

Sammy ran quickly back into the house. He ran past the sack of corn and began to open the cupboards, searching not for the corn but for food for himself.

There was a box of Wheaties in the cupboard, and Sammy turned it up and, eating from the box, walked over to the refrigerator. He unwrapped two slices of cheese, poured Wheaties on them, and washed it all down with water from the spigot.

There were apples on the window sill behind the sink, and Sammy had two of those, and then he took biscuits from a metal plate on the stove and ate those with more cheese. He was still standing at the refrigerator, eating, when he heard his grandfather.

"Boy, come on with the water. Hurry!"

Sammy swallowed the last of his biscuit. "I'm hurrying as fast as I can." He put the box of Wheaties in the refrigerator and closed the door. "Now, where is this corn anyway?" He moved to the sink to get one more apple.

Suddenly he got the feeling that someone was watching him. He glanced out the window and saw that his grandfather was still standing in the field with the crane. Sammy swirled around, and then he saw a small green parrot. It was perched on a mop handle which had been nailed across the corner of the kitchen. The parrot was watching him with its bright, beady eyes. It bobbed from side to side. Its eyes did not leave Sammy. Quickly, guiltily Sammy said, "I was just looking for the corn." Then he called louder, "Hey, where did you say the corn was?"

"In a sack by the door."

"Yeah, I see it now."

Sammy scooped up a handful of corn and grabbed the bucket of water as he went onto the porch. He ran across the yard, calling to his grandfather, "I would have been here sooner but I couldn't find the corn. It was behind the door."

He slowed down when he got to the gate and slipped through. "There's a parrot loose in your kitchen and it—" He stopped where he was. There was something about the way his grandfather was standing that bothered him. He waited. The bucket swung in one hand and stopped. The corn got sweaty in the other.

Sammy looked. The crane was still standing in the same place. His head was lifted, leaning a little to the left. He didn't seem any worse than when Sammy had left to get the corn. Still there was something wrong. Sammy had felt it instantly.

"What's wrong?" he asked.

His grandfather had his back to Sammy. His shoulders were sloping and his arms hung limply at his sides.

"What's wrong?" Sammy asked again. "Did something happen while I was in the house?" He left the gate. The bucket of water was a little heavier. "I got the corn." He opened his hand and held out the corn glistening with his sweat. His grandfather did not turn around to look.

Sammy took three steps through the weeds and he was standing in his grandfather's shadow. He set the bucket down. "What happened?" He had from earliest childhood hated not to know what was happening, and he was so persistent that no one had ever been able to keep anything from him. Now his voice rose with agitation and anxiety. "What's happened?"

His grandfather was shaking his head sadly from side to side. His neck bones creaked as he did this so that he seemed to be a machine that needed

88  oiling.

"What happened?"

His grandfather did not turn around. He lifted his hands and stuck them in his back belt loops. With his brown hands and white arms he appeared to be wearing gloves. He still shook his head in the same sad way.

"Are you deaf?" Sammy asked loudly. He remembered that there had been lots of times when his grandfather had not answered. He reached out and tugged the back of his grandfather's army pants. "Hey," he said loudly. "Hey, what happened?" He tugged harder. He was prepared to shake the answer out of his grandfather if necessary.

Then his grandfather turned and looked down at Sammy. In an old, gray voice he gave the explanation. "He's blind."

## BLIND!

Sammy could not believe he had heard correctly. "What did you say?" It was like the moment when he had learned that his parents had gone on to Detroit without him. There were some things that just didn't happen, and so the only explanation was that the ears had heard wrong.

"He's blind."

"The crane's blind?" His food was suddenly heavy in his stomach. He thought that each of those biscuits must have weighed five pounds.

"Yes, the crane is blind," his grandfather said.

Sammy could not speak. Silently he said, "Oh." There were some things that there was no answer to but that silent and painful "Oh." All the silent "Ohs" of Sammy's life began to flash in his mind. "Your dog's dead, Sammy, got run over on the highway." Oh. "You're not going to get your bicycle this Christmas." Oh. "Your parents have gone to Detroit without you." Oh. Moments later the words came—fast, hot words. "You're a liar. My dog's not dead!" Or "Who wants an old bicycle anyway?" Now he couldn't think of anything to say. Finally he stammered, "How could that happen though?"

His grandfather shook his head. "I thought there was something wrong the way he didn't run from us. Usually a crane's shy. It runs. And he held his head in a funny way—I don't know if you noticed it or not."

"No," Sammy said. "I never saw a crane before. I don't know how they are supposed to hold their heads."

"And his wings are battered. See, here? Like he'd been running into things again and again. I knew *something* was wrong, but . . ." His voice trailed off as if his strength had at last wound down.

Sammy said, "I didn't think birds got blind."

"Well, they don't live long if they do. A blind bird's not even a bird. He can't fly. He can't find food or water. He can't do nothing. He just waits and if he's lucky he dies fast."

"Maybe he's not blind though. You can never tell with a bird. Maybe—"

"Nature don't help a blind creature."

"But, listen, maybe—"

"Look at that." His grandfather put his hand up to the crane's head. "See? Nothing. No reaction at all. And you can look at the left eye and see it's injured." He motioned Sammy around so that he could see.

"How could that happen though?"

"He just ran into something most probably. All the injuries are on this side—the wing, the breast, the eye. From the looks of it, I'd say he flew into some electrical wires."

"But I see birds sitting on wires all the time. They practically live on wires."

"Yeah, but if a bird flies into the lead wire and hits another wire at the same time—and a bird the size of this crane could do that real easy—well, he could get a burn like this." He pointed to the bloody feathers on the bird's breast. "You see this here and here?" He pointed to the wing, the head.

Sammy nodded. "But why would the other eye be damaged?"

"Well, as I figure it from the look of that burn on his breast and wing, he hit right into the wires and there would be a flash in his face, an electrical flash, and it would be bright enough to burn his other eye. It would be like you staring into the sun for a while. It burns the eye." He shook his head sadly.

"Does that kind of burn clear up?"

"Sometimes if it's not too bad. Sometimes it don't ever get better." He paused, then added, "If it don't . . ."

"If it don't, what?" Sammy asked quickly.

"Nothing," his grandfather answered.

"No, I want to know—what? You wouldn't *kill* him."

His grandfather was a long time in answering. Finally he said, "I ain't going to keep a bird if it's in misery. Some things ain't right."

"But he's not miserable. How do you know he's miserable anyway?" Sammy answered. "It's only your opinion. *I* don't think he's miserable."

His grandfather looked out beyond the pen. "I'll tell you something, boy. Life turns out to be a lot more precious than you think. There ain't nothing more precious. It's like—"

"But what about the crane?"

"I'm coming around to the crane. First you look up there at the sky."

"But—"

94    "Look!" Squinting a little, Sammy looked up.

"You know what's up there, don't you?" his grandfather said.

Sammy looked and then glanced at his grandfather. "Clouds?"

"Beyond that. Beyond that," his grandfather continued without waiting for Sammy to answer, "is planets, boy, and then more planets and more planets. They say it goes on like that forever."

Sammy looked at his grandfather without speaking.

"And sometime, in your lifetime, boy, men are going to get up to the planets. They are going to get to planets you and me never even heard of. And you know what they're going to find?"

"What?"

"Nothing!" He clamped his mouth shut on the word. "They're going to find one dead planet after another, that's what I think. You'll be picking up the newspaper and reading one sorry headline after another. No life on Jupiter. No life on Mars. No life on this planet. No life on that planet. And not until you've seen every one of those headlines, not until you know there's not any life anywhere, *then*, boy, is when you'll know how precious life is." He glanced at the crane. "I know it right now just by being an old man, or I wouldn't have carried that

95

crane all the way home, and I'm not killing this crane if there's anything else I can do."

"There could be life on other planets."

"Yeah."

"But I guess there couldn't be too." Sammy shook his head. He said, "Well, anyway, I don't think he's all the way blind. He blinked his eye."

"We'll see." His grandfather waited, watching the crane. Then he straightened and said, "Well, give me the corn."

Sammy handed the corn to his grandfather, and his grandfather held it beneath the crane's beak, shaking it in his hand so that the crane could hear. The crane stood without moving. "He don't want to eat now. Corn was what he'd been after in that field, but he won't take it now."

"Keep trying," Sammy suggested.

"Give me the water." His grandfather lifted the bucket and sloshed the water around. He scratched his hand on the bottom of the bucket. The crane did not move, and Sammy's grandfather put the crane's head down into the water.

The crane drank. He lifted his head, swallowed, clapped his beak and then drank again.

"At least he's drinking," Sammy said. "He couldn't be completely miserable if he's drinking."

He looked at the crane, who had finished and was standing now with his head high, turned slightly toward them. Sammy felt the crane's stubborn will and was touched by it. He said, "I know he's going to be all right." He stepped forward, "Don't you think— His foot landed on one of the geese and the goose fluttered up, squawking. "I'm sorry," Sammy said absently, then to his grandfather, "Don't you think so?"

His grandfather turned without speaking and started walking toward the house. Sammy felt his question had been pointedly ignored. "The first thing to do," his grandfather said, "is to get some food in him—and in us too. I reckon you're hungry, boy, aren't you, not having any breakfast?"

Sammy felt a sudden stab of guilt and he turned slowly and walked behind his grandfather to the house. "Well, I'm not *that* hungry," he said.

"I made some biscuits for your folks for breakfast. There might be one or two of them left."

"I don't feel much like having a biscuit." This was the truth.

"Well, we'll find something."

They went into the kitchen and Sammy glanced first at the parrot in the corner, who was still there, quietly ruffling its feathers. He half expected the parrot to screech out his shame. The parrot would cry, "He already ate. He already ate." Sammy could almost hear the sharp mocking words. He cleared his throat and said, "Does your parrot talk much?"

"He says one or two things."

"Does he ever tell you things that have happened, anything like that?"

"No, he can say 'Where's Papa?' and—"

"Where's who?"

"Papa, that's me."

"Oh."

"And he can say 'Good-by,' only he don't know when to say it. Or else he just plain enjoys saying it at the wrong time. He won't ever tell somebody good-by when they're leaving. A thousand people could go out of this house and that parrot wouldn't say good-by to a one of them." He wiped his mustache in a gesture of disgust. "Folks say parrots don't know what they're saying, but that parrot does, because he just plain makes a point of saying good-by at the wrong time."

He went over and stood by the parrot. "Good-by, Paulie, good-by. I'm not going anywhere, so you can say it. Good-by. Good-by." He waited, then he gave up and crossed the kitche with his slow heavy steps. "I used to have me a fine gray parrot that knew all the parts of a car."

His grandfather paused to glance at the biscuit plate. He saw that the biscuits were gone and said, "Well, I'll fix us some spaghetti." He went into the pantry and the parrot said, "Good-by. Good-by."

"He said it!" Sammy cried.

"Yeah, he said it. He knows I'm in the pantry." He looked out at the parrot. "You don't say good-by when a person goes into the pantry." The parrot bobbed its head and began to walk sideways across the mop handle, circling the handle with its feet. "You say good-by when someone's going out the door. The *door!*" He pointed to the door and then disappeared into the pantry.

"Where's Papa?" the parrot screamed.

"You know where I am."

"Where's Papa?"

"He's in there," Sammy said. He sat down at the white table with the chipped porcelain top. He leaned forward on his arms. He remembered how much trouble it was to make spaghetti—his mother took all afternoon doing it—and so he said, "Don't go to any trouble on my account."

"It ain't no trouble." His grandfather came out of the pantry with a can of spaghetti in his hand. "Unless you want it heated."

"No, I don't want it heated," Sammy said

quickly. "I like it cold." He watched his grandfather open the can of spaghetti and divide it into two soup bowls. He wiped spoons off on a towel.

"Here you go."

Sammy took his bowl and set it down.

Suddenly his grandfather glanced up. "Here comes the owl," he said. "Remember I was telling you about him?"

Sammy had not heard anything. He looked around quickly and saw the owl flying to the back of the chair by the door. It was a silent mothlike flight. The owl rested there a moment and then swooped over to the table. The underside of his wings were white in the dark room. Startled, Sammy put up his hands. "He ain't going to hurt you," his grandfather said.

"I know that." The owl landed in the middle of the table and stood looking at Sammy. He stepped forward on his stiff legs and glared. He was a small owl, gray, about eight inches high, but he seemed bigger because of his large broad head and the ruff of feathers around his yellow eyes.

"He has eyelashes," Sammy said, "long ones." It was the first time he had seen an owl up close. "What is he looking at me for?" He laughed uneasily. "Have I got his bowl or something?"

His grandfather was bent over, eating. He ignored Sammy's question and said, "I figure we'll have to force-feed the crane at first." He shoveled spaghetti into his mouth like a man stoking a furnace. "We'll just make up a liquid mixture and pour it down."

"That's what I figured too." The geese were under the table. Their soft bodies rustled around Sammy's legs. He drew his feet behind him under the chair. The geese didn't bother him as much as the owl, who was still staring. Sammy said again, "What's the owl looking at me for?"

Spaghetti was beginning to stain his grandfather's mustache orange. He pointed at Sammy with his spoon and said, "We'll feed the crane as soon as we finish lunch. If he's blind, he hasn't been eating good."

The owl was gazing intently at Sammy. All of a sudden his head began to swing back and forth. He half raised his wings. Sammy said quickly, "But what's this owl up to? Is he going to do anything to me or what?"

"Don't worry about the owl. He's always coming up on something or somebody and getting them in his sight and staring at them for ten minutes or so and then flying off. He does that to the parrot. He

102

does that to my shoe. One time he stared at nothing in the corner of the room for fifteen minutes. It don't mean nothing."

The owl made a low noise. "Ooh."

Sammy said quickly, "Does *that* mean anything?"

"No. He'll get used to you."

The owl continued to stare. "Does he come to the table all the time?" Sammy asked.

"He'll come, but not to eat. He don't have any interest in food that don't move. He'll walk right across your plate." His grandfather looked at the owl and said, "His eyes are fixed. That's why he stares."

"I thought so."

"Watch here." His grandfather reached out and began to scratch the owl at the base of his bill. Slowly, contentedly, the owl closed both pairs of eyelids. "See that?"

"Yeah."

"That means he's real pleased. Sometimes he only closes the inner lids." He straightened and the owl opened his eyes and looked at Sammy. "Well, let's get to it." His grandfather took the last strand of sphaghetti from his bowl and held it out for the geese. One by one they came out from under the table to peck at it. One goose snapped it in half and ran. Another got the remainder, and the grandfather wiped his hands on his pants and said, "When you get finished, put your bowl and spoon over there in the sink. We got to keep things tidy."

"All right," Sammy said. He discovered that he had not even started to eat yet. With one eye on the owl, who was still staring at him with cold yellow eyes, Sammy ate quickly. As he ate he looked out the open door. He could see the crane in the pen. The crane was standing with his head tucked under his wing feathers.

Suddenly Sammy wasn't hungry any more. He took his remaining spaghetti and fed it cautiously to the geese, saying again and again, "Watch out for my fingers now, you guys. Watch out! Watch out!" He tried to make sure that the goose who was always hissing at him was not left out. "Watch out now. Give me room." Then he added quickly to the owl, "I'm just giving them some leftover spaghetti." The owl blinked once and continued to stare.

## THE OWL
## IN THE BATHROOM

After a moment the owl turned and walked stiff-legged across the table. He stood staring at the doorway, his knuckles curled down over the edge of the table.

"You see something?" Sammy asked. Sammy thought that the owl probably knew more about the inside of this house than his grandfather. He thought rooms would look different seen from the tops of doors and the insides of closets.

The owl stared through the doorway, then left the table and flew to the back of the chair by the door. Without pausing he flew out into the hall and onto the top of the front door. Then he glided down to the banister and kept flying in short swoops until he was upstairs.

Sammy listened to the owl fly away, then he got up and put the dishes in the sink. When his grandfather came out of the pantry, Sammy said, "The owl went upstairs somewhere. I don't know what he's up to."

Sammy's grandfather was making a mixture of mashed sardines, meal, canned milk, and water. "I think this will do the trick," he said to Sammy as he stirred. He had put his old railroad jacket back on, and he looked more like himself. He mixed the sardines and mopped his jacket with one hand when his enthusiastic stirring caused some to spill.

Sammy walked over and looked into the bowl. When he was a little boy he had spent a lot of time mixing things together—just mixing different foods to see how they tasted, and then he wouldn't have the nerve to try them. He would go around begging people, "Taste this for me and tell me what it's like," and they would always say, "You taste it yourself."

He hoped his grandfather wasn't going to ask him to taste this particular mixture. He sighed and said, "That spaghetti really filled me up." His grandfather added more sardines. Sammy said, "I couldn't eat another bite of *anything* I'm so full."

"Well, let's get to it." His grandfather turned and Sammy followed him out into the yard.

As they went down the steps Sammy asked, "Where does the owl go upstairs? Do you know?"

"The owl? He's got a favorite place in the bathroom up on a pipe, and he likes the top part of one of the closets. He could be 'most anywhere up there, I reckon." They crossed the yard together. "He goes in the back bedroom sometimes because there's a mirror on the dresser and he likes to look at himself."

"Is that the truth?"

"I caught him at it once, swooping down at himself and then landing and walking past. He's got a kind of hop he does. You ever seen an owl walk?"

"No, I just saw him take a couple of steps on the table."

"Well, he hobbles along with his head bowed and his wings drooping. He's more like an old man thinking about something than a bird. Anyway, he'd walk past the mirror and then he'd fly up and swoop down at himself and then land and walk past."

"I never knew birds could see themselves in a mirror."

"I had a thrasher used to attack himself." His grandfather paused. "'Course with the owl, it's more admiration. Or maybe he gets lonesome. I don't know." He kept walking. "I reckon we'll have to let him go before long, but it would surprise you, boy, how much you can miss an owl or a blackbird once it's lived with you."

"I would miss the owl already."

His grandfather stopped talking as they went through the gate. Sammy could see that the crane was still in the same place, standing without moving, his head rising above the fence like a periscope.

The afternoon was hot and quiet. The only sound was the noise the geese made rustling through the weeds as they followed Sammy's grandfather into the pen. "I'll open his beak and you pour the food in, hear? Let it run down the side of his throat," his grandfather said. "We don't want to choke him."

The geese stopped at the gate and stood like a small inattentive audience. One goose left the group and went over to attack a weed by the fence post. When she had reduced it to tatters she spread her wings proudly and came back to join the others.

Sammy stood on one side of the crane and looked at his grandfather. The sun was in his eyes and he blinked. He said, "I don't know if I'm going to be able to do this right or not."

"Over to the side of his throat now," his grandfather said, as if Sammy had not spoken.

"I said that I don't know whether I can—" His grandfather cut off his words by thrusting the bowl into his hands.

"Here."

Sammy took the bowl uneasily. "I don't know whether I can or not," he said again. There was some of the mixture on the outside of the bowl, and the bowl was so slick Sammy almost dropped it. He got it steady and glanced at his grandfather.

"Now," his grandfather said.

The crane did not put up a struggle at first. He allowed his beak to be opened, but as soon as Sammy shakily put a spoonful of the sardine liquid into his throat, he rebelled. He closed his gullet and most of the mixture came out and ran down the outside of his throat. His neck was pale and seemed thin and fragile. Sammy tried to wipe away the mixture with the side of his hand.

"Don't bother about that," his grandfather said. "That won't hurt him. Just try to get it into his mouth this time."

"I told you I wasn't going to be able to do it," Sammy said. He let another spoonful dribble down the inside of the crane's throat. The crane swallowed.

"You're doing all right," his grandfather said. "Just keep going."

After the first few spoonfuls the crane seemed to give up and accept the indignity of the feeding. "Now, that ought to do it," his grandfather said finally, and Sammy gratefully let the spoon plop back into the liquid.

His grandfather took the bucket of water and began to wash some of the food and dirt from the crane's feathers. Sammy wiped his hands on his pants. He looked back at the house. After a minute he asked, "Now, where is it that owl hides out?"

"In the bathroom generally."

"Well, I thought I might just go up there and have a look," Sammy said casually.

"Take him something. He likes moths or grasshoppers, anything in that line." Sammy hesitated and his grandfather said, "Everywhere you step around here there's a grasshopper, boy, just look around."

Sammy walked around the yard for a while, his eyes on the ground. Finally he found a grasshopper in the high grass by the back porch and caught it on the third try. "Is this kind all right?" he asked his grandfather.

His grandfather nodded. "Wait a minute. Let me have that." He took the grasshopper from Sammy and held it up to the crane. There was no reaction. His grandfather waited a minute and then handed the grasshopper back to Sammy. "I don't reckon he's hungry now," he said in a disappointed voice.

With the grasshopper wiggling in his hand, Sammy went slowly into the house and up the stairs. The top floor of the house was tidier than the first floor. No mud had been tracked up here and the geese rarely came up the stairs. All the furniture was in place and the beds were covered with spreads.

Sammy walked cautiously down the hall and into the bathroom. The linoleum was cool beneath his feet and all the spigots dripped a little, making a pleasant rhythmic sound. Vines grew over the windows so that no sun ever came in, and the bathroom was as dark and cool as the forest. Sammy thought that it was no wonder the owl liked it up here.

He stopped in the middle of the room and looked up. An old shower curtain, torn and sagging, was pushed against the wall, and there was a shelf behind the curtain with old hair-tonic bottles on it. Just under the shelf on the shower pipe was the owl. The owl's head was turned toward Sammy. His yellow eyes looked unblinkingly at him.

Sammy said, "I brought you something." He put

the grasshopper down into the tub. "This is yours." He backed away slowly.

The owl kept watching Sammy. He blinked his eyes once, his lower lids moving up to meet the top lids, and then he turned his head and looked down into the tub.

The tub was stained with rust where the water dripped, and the dust of several years lay in the bottom. The grasshopper, at the far end of the tub, began hopping up against the side and falling back.

The owl's look intensified. His pupils snapped open. He strained upward, and then suddenly he bobbed from side to side, swaying, his eyes on the grasshopper. He leaned forward. His talons tightened on the shower pipe. His eyes seemed to pierce the grasshopper. The grasshopper jumped again and fell back into the tub.

Sammy was holding his breath. His eyes went from the owl to the grasshopper.

The owl was motionless now. His stare was fixed. The grasshopper leaped one more time and fell back. It remained in the corner of the tub. Both the owl and the grasshopper were motionless then.

The owl made a faint hissing sound, like steam escaping. Then he swooped down into the tub and pounced on the grasshopper with both feet.

His talons curled around the grasshopper, and he put it in his mouth.

The owl's mouth seemed enormous when he opened it, and Sammy stood silently watching him eat. When the owl finished he flew back to the shower pipe and turned his head to Sammy.

Sammy was standing there with his mouth hanging open. He was thinking that this house had everything—geese, a parrot in the kitchen, a crane, and an owl in the bathroom.

Then suddenly Sammy noticed how intently the owl was staring at him. He took a step backward. He said quickly, "That was the only one I could find." He backed out into the hall and went quietly down the stairs.

## NIGHT COMES

$S$ammy and his grandfather force-fed the crane again after supper, but the crane still made no effort to help. He just allowed himself to be fed after a brief struggle.

Sammy's grandfather stood looking at the ruffled, battered crane, then he looked down in the bowl at the remaining food and he sighed. "Them cranes I used to know could eat a hundred and fifty grasshoppers in the morning and a hundred and fifty at night. That's a hundred and fifty *each*." He shook his head. "This don't look good."

"His not eating?"

His grandfather answered, "Everything don't look good." It was a judgment. "Not eating, not caring, not trying to get away, not doing nothing."

"I don't guess there's any way to *make* him want to live," Sammy said.

"You know, that's a funny thing. I got me three

wild ducklings one time—my dog brought one home and then went back and got two more, just carried them home in his mouth. Anyway, two of them ducks lived and grew up and the other one just died. There wasn't any reason I could see. Two just lived and one didn't."

"Oh." Sammy looked away from the crane and then up at the sky. He watched the color fade out of the sky, and he felt as if he were fading out in the same way. He was very tired. He thought he was going to fall asleep standing in the pen. He remembered an old man who had lived behind his family in Alabama. This old man would fall asleep standing on the sidewalk waiting to cross the street. Sammy understood now how that could happen. He had almost fallen asleep at the supper table and then again when he was sitting on the back steps and now in the pen. He looked at his grandfather and said, "What time do you go to bed around here?"

His grandfather looked surprised at the question. "Well, whenever you want to."

Sammy nodded. That was the way it was at home. He never had to go to bed there as long as he didn't bother anybody.

"You can go on to bed now if you're tired."

"No, I'm not tired," he said quickly.

"Well, whenever you want to then. It don't matter."

Sammy stood in the weeds, waiting. He scratched the back of one leg with his foot. His grandfather waited too. He took off his hat, combed his hair with his hand, and settled that hat back in the same place. Even the geese at the gate, facing in different directions, still as statues, were waiting.

"Well," his grandfather said, "don't look like he's going to do anything tonight."

"No," Sammy agreed. He yawned, hid it behind his hand, and said, "Well, maybe I might just go in and lie down for a minute or two."

"You go ahead. I put your suitcase in your room."

Sammy went into the bedroom, lay down on the bed, and stretched out his aching legs. His legs were so dusty that he appeared to have on stockings.

Sammy had never been known for his cleanliness, but he could never remember being this dirty before in his life. He even felt dirty. He wished suddenly that his old teacher Mrs. Haggendorn could see him. Mrs. Haggendorn had tried to get him clean the whole time he was in her room. The third grade, as he looked back on it, seemed to have been one long struggle against being clean.

Once on his report card she had written, "Sammy

needs to work on his personal hygiene." Sammy had asked his mother, "What does that mean?" And his brother had hollered from the bedroom, "It means you're filthy."

"I am not filthy!" he had said. "A little dirty maybe sometimes, but I'm not filthy, Mom."

"You call that a little dirty?" his mother had cried, noticing him closely for the first time in weeks. She turned him around so she could see the back of his neck. "And let me see your hands." Reluctantly he had shown them to her. "Now, those *are* filthy, Sammy. What does the teacher think of me letting you go around like that?"

"She doesn't think anything."

"When's the last time you washed those hands?"

"I don't know."

"Yesterday?"

"Yes, either then or this morning."

"Well, I know it wasn't this morning," his mother said. "And what's that in the center of your hand?"

It was a picture of the Titanic drawn with Magic Marker, but he didn't want to tell her that because she had helped him do his report on the Titanic a week ago and that would date his hand washing. He said, "It looks like Magic Marker."

"Well, go right in there now and get it off. Take a bath, Sammy. I mean it."

For a while after that she had kept after him about being clean and his father even brought home some special cleanser in a can that the men at the garage used to get out stubborn dirt and grease. Then after a week, his mother had stopped noticing and he had stopped washing.

He lifted one leg and looked at it. Even his mother would notice now, he thought, but his grandfather hadn't. After supper Sammy had half expected his grandfather to say, "Well, get your bath now." Sammy had wondered what the owl would think when he went into the bathroom and put water in the tub. He didn't think anybody had done that for years. It would be a big surprise for the owl to see what a tub was really used for.

His grandfather had said nothing. He had glanced down at Sammy's bare feet and not even noticed the dirt. Then, as if he had read part of Sammy's mind, he had turned and said to the parrot, "Want a bath, Paulie?"

"Paulie?" Sammy had said. Paulie was the cleanest thing in the house.

His grandfather went over, put out his hand, and the parrot stepped on to his index finger. "He loves a shower, don't you, Paulie?"

"Good-by," Paulie screeched. "Good-by."

"He thinks he's going somewhere," Sammy said.

"No, he don't." His grandfather set the parrot in the sink and turned on a trickle of water. The parrot began to flutter his wings and splash, to dip his head around under the water.

Sammy said, "Does the owl ever take a bath?"

"He used to be in the habit of drinking out of a blue bowl every evening, and one night it was hot and he just stepped into the bowl and bathed as nice as a pigeon. Owls don't bathe much though because they can't fly when they're wet. It takes them fifteen or twenty minutes to get dried out." He waited a few minutes while the parrot showered. Then he said, "Had enough, Paulie?" and carried him back to his perch.

Sammy closed his eyes and lay with his arms and legs spread out. He waited to fall asleep. He turned over and resettled himself, but the thought of the crane kept coming into his mind to keep him awake. He flipped over onto his back. After a few minutes he turned on his side.

He heard his grandfather in the hall and he called out, "What time is it anyway?"

There was a pause. "It's about ten o'clock, I reckon."

Sammy thought that his grandfather must tell

time by the sun and the stars because he had not seen a clock in the house. "Well, I'll probably go on to sleep now."

"Do what you want."

Sammy turned over again and closed his eyes. The sharp face of the crane rose in his mind. He could not understand why he cared about the crane. "It's just a bird," he told himself, the way he used to tell himself, "It's just a movie," when he was alone at night watching television, a movie like *The Last Man on Earth* or *The Mummy*. "It's just a movie" never made him feel less afraid then, and saying "It's just a bird" didn't make him care less now.

He waited and then called, "What time is it *now*?" His grandfather paused and answered, "Oh, it's ten-thirty or so."

"What are you doing outside?" Sammy asked quickly. "Is the crane all right?" His grandfather did not answer immediately, but after a minute he passed Sammy's window. Sammy sat up and asked, "Has something happened to the crane?"

"No, I just caught a moth for the owl. He likes these hawk moths." He held up his closed hand and walked on around to the back door.

Sammy lay down again. He thought he would lie there until the back door opened. Then he would get up and go into the kitchen and see the owl eat the moth. Sammy wanted to see the owl catch the moth in flight, just swoop down from the top of the door and scoop it up in his beak. His grandfather had said the owl had done that once or twice, but he wasn't very good at it. Even with a big mouth and whiskers to help, it was still hard for the owl to catch something in the air. Anyway, Sammy thought he would like to see him try.

Sammy turned to his side and watched the door. The owl went past, gliding silently down the hall. Although Sammy was watching, he wouldn't have seen the owl except for the white underpart of his wings.

Sammy got up and went out the door. He was so sleepy he had to feel his way down the hall. "I'm coming," he called to his grandfather. "Don't give him the moth yet."

Sammy came into the kitchen and his grandfather was standing by the table. On top of the open door was the owl. "I'm here," Sammy said.

Sammy's grandfather opened his hand and threw the moth into the air. It fluttered around the light and then flew over to the wall. The owl saw the moth instantly. He stared. He leaned forward on the top of the door.

The moth was resting halfway up the wall. Its

wings were folded back, the front part of its body was raised. The owl waited to make sure the moth was settled, and then he came down in one graceful swoop. He might have been soaring down from the heights of an old oak tree in the dark of night. He took the moth in flight, grabbing it in one claw, and then he flew out into the hall with it.

"Second time I've ever seen him do it with one hand!" his grandfather cried.

"Yah!" said Sammy tiredly.

Sammy turned, staggered back down the hall, fell on the bed, and was sound asleep as soon as his head hit the pillow.

## GREEN CREEK

Sammy awoke in the morning and got out of bed quickly. He looked out the window. On this side of the house the weeds grew thickest, and here his grandfather had put discarded items—an old rusted truck with no tires, a sink that held enough water for a birdbath, wooden crates, broken chairs, an old iron bed.

Closer to the house was a small garden, and his grandfather had told Sammy they would have to guard the tomato plants later in the year because the turtles in this part of the country loved tomatoes. Every summer, his grandfather said, he lost half his tomatoes to turtles.

"I can guard the tomatoes for you," Sammy had said.

"Well, I'd appreciate it."

Now Sammy thought about walking down the

row of tomatoes, spotting a turtle who was helping himself. "Aha, got you!" He would carry the turtle away, take him to where there was something to eat, but not tomatoes.

Suddenly Sammy remembered the crane. He turned and started into the kitchen. He had not bothered to put on his pajamas the night before and so was now already dressed for the day. In the kitchen one of the geese was sitting in a little patch of sunlight. The parrot was on his perch in the corner. The owl was absent.

Sammy went to the window. He could see his grandfather standing by the pen, but he could not see the crane. He leaned against the window sill, peering out. He wanted to call and ask how the crane was, but he was suddenly afraid the crane had died during the night. He did not want to call, "How's the crane?" if the answer was going to be "Dead."

He waited at the window for a minute. Behind him the parrot said, "Where's Papa?" in a loud screech.

Sammy turned around. His face brightened. He said, "He's outside."

"Where's Papa?"

"Outside. Papa's outside." Sammy waited, then
he remembered the crane and turned back to the

window. His grandfather had shifted to one side, and now Sammy could see that the crane was still there, standing in the shade, his head turned as if he were looking over the fence. Relieved, Sammy went and sat at the table.

"Good-by," the parrot screeched.

Sammy glanced at him in disgust. "I'm not going anywhere."

"Where's Papa?"

"Outside."

"Where's Papa?"

"I already told you. *Outside*. Now, I'm not answering any more."

"Where's Papa?"

"I'm not *answering*." He turned his back on the parrot and sat at the table. His grandfather had made biscuits for breakfast, big round flat ones that looked like hard pancakes, and Sammy put jelly on two of them and drank some water. This jelly, Sammy's grandfather had told him at supper the night before, was twelve years old. It had been stored up in one of the bedroom closets and been forgotten. Then one night the grandfather heard noises upstairs. He had gone up the next morning to see what the trouble was, and when he went into this one bedroom he saw a terrible mess. Jelly was everywhere. The bedspread was covered with it, and there were empty jars on the floor with the sealing wax pulled out. In the middle of the bed a raccoon was lying fast asleep, and his stomach was bulging with jelly. It was as round as a melon. He had come in the open window and eaten five jars of jelly. His grandfather was glad it happened though, because that was how he had found the other six jars of jelly the raccoon didn't open. He had saved them for a special occasion.

"Good-by," the parrot screeched.

"Good-by yourself." Sammy finished eating, got another drink of water, and went out into the yard. He walked to where his grandfather was standing, leaning against the fence, looking at the crane.

"How's he doing?" Sammy asked.

His grandfather shook his head. "The same. He don't want to eat. Don't want to do nothing. I forced a little food down him." His grandfather had a stick in his mouth and he took it out, showed it to Sammy, and said, "Want one? It's a cherry twig."

Sammy said, "No."

"It's the best toothbrush there is. If they put these in boxes they couldn't keep them on the drugstore shelves. I wouldn't use no other toothbrush."

"Oh, well, I'll try one." Sammy thought that it would save him the trouble of opening his suitcase.

His grandfather broke him off a twig, and

Sammy frayed it on one end the way his grandfather had done and stuck it in his mouth. Then he leaned over the fence like his grandfather. They didn't speak for a minute. Sammy glanced up at his grandfather and started to tell him about the conversation he had had with the parrot, but he stopped. His grandfather looked so old that Sammy was startled. He said, "How old are you?" His grandfather seemed beyond years.

His grandfather didn't answer. Then, still staring at the crane, he said, "Sometimes I get the feeling that I'm a god."

"A what?" Sammy had been busy trying to figure out how old his grandfather was, but when he heard that he straightened and said, "A what?"

"A god, you know, a *god!*" His grandfather made a big expansive gesture in the air.

It was something Sammy had never thought of his grandfather as being, but he said, "Oh, well sure." He stuck the toothbrush back in his mouth.

"Like right now I got the feeling that if I went over there and I set my hands on that crane, and if I said, 'Crane, *live,*' well, I feel like the power would go out of me right through my hands and into that crane like electricity and that crane *would* live. That's the way I feel."

"I've felt like that."

"Only it don't work."

"I know."

"I've tried it."

Sammy hesitated, then said, "Me too."

"I mean I've actually put my hands on an animal. That's how big a fool I am. I mean I actually put my hands on a horse named Buddy one time. I actually said, 'Buddy, *live.*' And I wanted that horse to live so bad I half expected it to work." He held his hands stretched out in front of him, wide enough to cover a horse's back. "I done the same thing to my gray parrot. I come in the kitchen one morning and my parrot was standing in the sink—there was a little water in there. He never had done that before and I knew he was sick. I done everything I could for that parrot and when there was nothing else to do and I knew my parrot was dying, I put my hands on him and said, 'Parrot, live.'" He let his hands drop to his sides. "It just plain don't work."

"It didn't work on my dog."

"Which is too bad, ain't it, boy?"

Sammy nodded.

"It would be a good thing if we could have things the way we wanted them, huh, boy?"

"Yeah."

His grandfather sighed and straightened. He put

his hands on his back. Then he shook his shoulders beneath the old railroad jacket and said, "Well, I was thinking we'd take the crane down to the creek. It's nice down there and a crane's a water bird. It might help him."

"Do birds sometimes just perk up suddenly? I mean, do they do poorly at first and then all of a sudden just perk up? Did the owl do that?"

"Not the owl. He never give me any trouble. Oh, he don't see too good at close range and he didn't eat for that reason—he just plain couldn't see what I was giving him. When I got food up close enough to touch his whiskers, well, he ate it. He never turned down anything I brought him except a toad and a caterpillar."

"Did the crow give you any trouble?"

"No."

"The ducks?"

"No. 'Course none of them was blind." His grandfather started into the pen. "Well, let's get him down to the creek." Then he turned to Sammy and said, "You get my fishing pole off the back porch."

Sammy hurried. His brother had told him about Green Creek. His brother had said it was the best fishing creek in the world. There was long grass on the bottom, and fish darted up and down like torpedoes, making parts in the long grass as they swam. His brother had said that if you were quick, you could scoop them up with a net.

"Here I am," Sammy said.

His grandfather, carrying the crane, nodded and walked slowly in front of Sammy toward the creek. When they were halfway through the trees the geese came to join them, running until they caught up and then following along behind in single file. The geese took a short cut through some weeds and only their long necks were visible. Then they came back to the path again and took their place between Sammy and his grandfather.

The breeze ruffled their pale feathers. Sammy watched them and said, "Those geese are nice walkers." In his admiration he caught the tip of the fishing pole in the leaves overhead and stopped to shake it free.

"Yeah," his grandfather said without looking around, "they got longer legs than ducks."

Sammy got the fishing pole free and hurried to catch up with the geese and his grandfather. "They don't even waddle much."

His grandfather said, "My grandmother—she came to this country when she was a girl—she told me once that she used to have to walk the geese to market. That was her job. And she said they used to make the geese walk through sticky tar first and then walk through sand because that would coat their feet and protect them like shoes. I don't reckon people do that any more. They just drive the geese to market in trucks."

"Still, they're nice walkers. They *could* walk to market if they had to."

"Sometimes I'll be walking two miles toward Gatsburg where some apple trees are and I'll hear a rustling and the geese will come filing out of the weeds. Or up at the Hunter place where I get nuts —I'll look up and they'll be strolling down the road. It surprises you where those geese go."

They got to the creek, and the geese slipped down the bank and noiselessly moved into the water. At once they began turning upside down, reaching into the grass that grew on the bottom of the creek. When they lifted their heads they clacked their bills, sifting what they had found.

Sammy's grandfather set the crane down in the water, and Sammy stood on the bank, holding the fishing pole in one hand. The crane remained motionless. He was a pitiful sight. Sammy's grandfather had bound up his crippled wing the night before. It was now held in place with strips of old brown cloth, and his feathers were rumpled and wind-blown. He looked, Sammy thought, like a package that had been poorly wrapped and had come loose in the mail.

The crane continued to stand in the water. The current moved so slowly that the water seemed to be still, but the grass was bent in the bottom of the creek and the geese were beginning to drift a little downstream.

Suddenly the crane took two steps forward in the water, picking his way stiffly on his long thin legs. It was the first time he had walked since his capture, and Sammy held his breath.

The geese were a flurry of activity. They had found something under the water and they were diving, digging with their bills, splashing. But it was the crane, just taking a few steps in the water, that held Sammy's attention.

The crane hesitated. He cocked his head to one side. Then he put his bill into the water and drank. He lifted his head and swallowed. He took another stiff step and drank again.

"Yonder's a frog," his grandfather said. "See it, over there by the other bank, floating on the water? Get over there and catch it."

Sammy started wading across the creek. The grass

curled around his feet, and in the middle of the stream the water began to get deep. "Hey, my clothes are going to get wet."

"They'll dry."

"How deep is this water anyway?"

"Swim if you want to."

"No, I'll just keep wading," Sammy said. He had never learned to swim. He could manage to stay on top of the water by slapping his arms and pumping his feet so hard the water was almost whipped into the air. But he could only keep this up for about a minute, and then he got so tired he sank. When anyone asked him if he could swim he gave them a disgusted look and said, "Naturally." Now he added, "I don't want to swim because I'm afraid I'll frighten the frog away."

"Well, just wade over quietly then."

In the center of the stream the water was up to Sammy's waist. He felt a fish dart in front of his feet and he said, "There's something down there."

"Keep your eye on the frog."

"I am, but there's something down there." He kept trudging through the water. Green dragonflies darted around him. He could see the frog floating on the water by a rock, its front feet touching the edge of the rock. Sammy came forward slowly, silently. Then he reached down in one swoop, grabbed the

frog, and lifted him in the air. "Got him!" he cried.

"Now give it to the crane."

Slowly Sammy waded back across the stream to where the crane was standing in the water. He hesitated. "How do I do this?"

"Hold it up to his bill. Wiggle it by one foot. Let him know what you've got."

Sammy dangled the frog in front of the crane. "I don't think he wants it."

"He don't know about it yet," his grandfather said. *"Make* him want it."

Sammy dipped the frog down into the water and held it up again, touching the crane's beak. He waited. He said again, "I don't think he wants it."

"Don't give up."

"Does it look like I'm giving up?" Sammy said. He looked back at the crane. He said, "I'll stand here all day if I have to."

## THE BEGINNING

When Sammy was a little boy, there were times when the world slowed down, times when the world moved so slowly Sammy wanted to fall to his knees and press his ear to the earth like it was a giant watch and see if it was still ticking. Then there were times when the world moved so fast he felt he could be spun off into space. Now, as he dangled the frog in front of the crane, the world seemed to have stopped.

He did not look at his grandfather, but he knew that the world had stopped for him too. His grandfather was balanced halfway down the bank, one foot set awkwardly in front of the other.

Sammy dipped the frog into the water again and held it up dripping wet. The crane did not notice. Sammy put it down into the water and splashed it about.

137

Then suddenly the crane jerked his head forward. He peered down into the water. Sammy swished the frog back and forth. The crane hesitated, his head cocked to the side. He moved his head closer to the water. Then he dipped his long beak down into the water and took the frog from Sammy's fingers.

With a click the world started up again. "He took it!" Sammy cried.

The crane threshed the frog around in the water with his beak. Then he tossed the frog back into his bill and swallowed.

"He ate it whole," Sammy said.

Sammy's grandfather stumbled down the bank and caught himself just at the edge of the water by grabbing a small tree. He lowered himself to the bank and sat. His old boots with the sides cut out were dug into the sand. He smoothed his mustache with his fingers, his eyes on the crane. Sammy waded over and sat down beside him.

The crane moved farther out into the stream. He dropped into the water and immersed himself. Only his head and neck were above the water, and then he rose and shook himself. He went in the water again. He paddled for a moment, swimming like the geese. Then he moved to the opposite shore and began dipping his bill into the bank.

"He's after something," Sammy's grandfather said.

Feeling with his beak, the crane probed the bank and began working a root out of the damp soil. "There'll be insects around the bottom of them roots," Sammy's grandfather said. "I reckon that's what he's after."

The crane probed and dug, worked out the root, ate the grubs that came with it, and then ate the root itself. He dug several inches, exposed another root, and ate it. Then he began drilling with his beak into the muddy creek bottom.

"He's going to make it," Sammy said. It was the first time he had said this and really believed it. He looked at his grandfather for confirmation.

He waited while his grandfather took off his hat, scratched his head, and put the hat back on. "He'll make it," his grandfather said.

Sammy let all the air go out of his body, and when the new air came in, he felt very good. He said, "I'll try to find him another frog." He got up and began wading up the creek. "You catch some fish for him and I'll be in charge of the frogs."

As Sammy walked through the water, he suddenly thought about his parents. They were probably in Detroit now. He looked back at the crane, 139 who was pulling roots out of the bank again. Then he looked at his grandfather. The shade from the trees made a lacy pattern on his dusty clothes.

Sammy waded out in the deeper water and stood for a minute. He looked down at his wet clothes, and he suddenly had a pleasant thought. He thought that when he went to Detroit to join his parents, all his clothes would still be in the suitcase, folded and clean, just the way they were now. He would wear this same outfit all summer and clean it in the creek. It would be a nice surprise for his mother.

He glanced down the creek to where the geese were resting in the green shadows of a low tree. He looked back at his grandfather, who was doing something to his fishing pole. He said, "You want to see me swim, Papa?"

His grandfather set his fishing pole down and looked at him. "Go ahead, boy."

Sammy stood in the water. He kept looking at his grandfather. He blinked and shaded his eyes with one hand so he could see his grandfather a little clearer.

Suddenly Sammy wanted his grandfather to know him the way he knew his birds. He wanted his grandfather to be able to pick him out of a thousand boys the way he could pick out the blackbird, the owl, the wild ducks. He wanted his grandfather to include him in his losses one day. He wanted his grandfather to say, "The blackbird's gone out into the world. The owl's gone. The crane flew off one day. The wild ducks are gone." Then he wanted his grandfather to add in the same sad voice, "Sammy's gone too."

Sammy kept looking at his grandfather in a funny way. He didn't know how it was possible to hate a person in the middle of one morning, and then to find in the middle of the next morning that you loved this same person.

His grandfather said, "Go ahead, boy, I'm looking."

Sammy cleared his throat. He said, "My name's Sammy."

His grandfather nodded. "Sammy," he said. "Go ahead, Sammy, let's see you swim."

Sammy remained without moving for a moment. He was intense. He breathed deeply. He stretched out his arms. He took another deep breath. Then he pushed himself off, and in a blaze of water he began to slap his arms, to struggle with his feet.

Startled by the confusion in the water, the geese rose and moved back in the shadows. The crane made a quick movement with his free wing. He lifted his head, took two steps, and hesitated.

Sammy came up and wiped the water out of his eyes. "How was that?"

"Fine," his grandfather said kindly. "That was fine, Sammy."

"I can't do it very well now, but I'll get better. Right now I'm going to find another frog." He moved back to the bank. He felt good and clean at last. He smoothed his red hair down on his head. "I'll get better. Don't you worry about that."

Up ahead he saw a frog on the bank. He cried, "I see one!" Then he waded quickly and quietly through the water to catch it.

## About the Author

BETSY BYARS was born in Charlotte, North Carolina, and lived there until her graduation from Queens College.

The mother of four, Mrs. Byars began writing books for children as her own family was growing up. She is the author of many books, including Puffin Story Books *The 18th Emergency* and *The Midnight Fox*. Mrs. Byars received the Newbery Award for *The Summer of the Swans*.

Mrs. Byars now lives in South Carolina, where her husband is associated with Clemson University. She and her husband have traveled widely throughout the United States in pursuit of their interest in gliding and antique airplanes.